Contents

VISUAL BASIC .NET

in easy steps

on or before

TIM ANDERSON

In easy steps is an imprint of Computer Step
Southfield Road . Southam
Warwickshire CV47 OFB . England

http://www.ineasysteps.com

Notice of Liability

Every effort has been made to ensure that this book contains accurate
and current information. However, Computer Step and the author shall
not be liable for any loss or damage suffered by readers as a result of
any information contained herein.

Trademarks

Microsoft® and Windows® are registered trademarks of Microsoft
Corporation. All other trademarks are acknowledged as belonging to
their respective companies.

Printed and bound in the United Kingdom

ISBN 1-84078-131-9

Getting Started

This chapter gives an overview of Visual Basic, including the differences between available versions: the standalone Standard edition, or one of the three Visual Studio .Net packages.

Covers

Chapter One

Introduction

Visual Basic is the easy way to write programs for Windows and the Internet. But why write a program? Simply, because it gives you the maximum control over your computer. Programs can automate your work, preventing mistakes and making you more productive. Programming is fun as well!

Writing programs can be complex, but fortunately Visual Basic makes it easy to get started. You can choose how far to go. Another advantage of Visual Basic is that it works with other applications like Microsoft Office and Corel WordPerfect, although Visual Basic .Net is a different version of the language.

There are several versions of Visual Basic available:

- Visual Basic Standard Edition is ideal for beginners. Everything you need to create Windows programs is included

- Visual Studio .Net includes an enhanced version of Visual Basic as well as other languages like C++, C#, and the Java-like J#. The Professional Edition is a complete development bundle

- Visual Studio .Net Enterprise Developer adds features like source code control, and comes with development versions of Windows server products. The Enterprise Architect version adds modelling tools and other high-end features

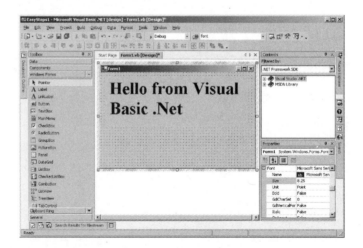

Visual Basic is programming for everyone

Visual Basic and Visual Basic .Net

Although it has the old "Visual Basic" name, the .Net version is really a brand new language.

Visual Basic .Net is not just the latest upgrade to Visual Basic. It is a new language with so many differences from earlier versions that compatibility has been lost. The good news is that it is superior in many ways. The bad news is that even experienced VB programmers have some learning to do.

Here are some of the reasons why it is worth moving to the .Net version:

- Programming powerful Web applications is almost as easy as programming for Windows

- Like most modern languages, but unlike the old VB, Visual Basic .Net is fully object-oriented. What this means is explained on page 52. It also makes VB a good language for learning how to program, whereas the old version is getting rather dated

- Visual Basic .Net is equally as powerful as other languages such as C++ or C#, whereas the old Visual Basic had limitations at the highest levels

To run Visual Basic .Net you need Windows NT 4.0, 2000 or XP. It does not run on Windows 95, 98 or Me.

- Visual Basic .Net is part of the .Net Framework. This gives you access to a rich set of components and other functions, as well as providing security and reliability features. Microsoft calls this "Managed code", meaning that the .Net runtime manages the security, memory usage, and performance optimisation of your program

To complete the picture, there are still reasons why you might want to use the old VB. It runs on lower-powered hardware, and you can build applications for Windows 95, which Visual Basic .Net does not support. Overall, the message is to use VB 6.0 if you have to, but VB .Net if you can. It really is better.

Installing Visual Basic

Installing Visual Basic (or the complete Visual Studio) is a matter of running setup from the first CD in your installation pack and following the directions, which will vary according to what is already installed on your machine.

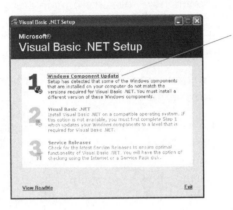

You may need to install the Component Update. This is a set of system files used both by Visual Basic and other Windows software.

If you are not sure about whether to install a Web server, continue without it. Visual Basic will still work, and you can install a Web server later if you want. If you are on a network, there may be a Web server on another machine you can use instead. The reason for caution is that running a Web server can be a security risk when you connect to the Internet.

2 With Visual Basic you can build powerful Web applications. These require a Web server, so you have the option to install one on your own machine. If you do this, pay careful attention to the security notes. Otherwise, just click Continue: Visual Basic will still work, and you can install the Web server later if you want.

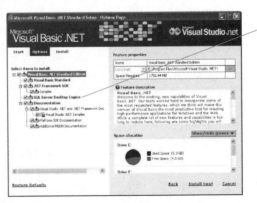

3 Select which components you need. The documentation takes a lot of space. Uncheck some of the options if you need to.

Making sense of the IDE

To run Visual Basic, run Microsoft Visual Studio .NET from the Programs group of the Start menu.

When you run Visual Basic, it opens up in an application called an IDE, which stands for "Integrated Development Environment." This consists of a central work area surrounded by tool windows and with a menu and toolbars at the top. The docked tool windows can be "torn off" as floating windows, or hidden altogether. You can also have them partially hidden, so they pop out when the mouse clicks their button at the border of the IDE. This is called an Auto Hide window. The central work area is tabbed, and the tabs can take you to both visual designers like the form editor, and text editors.

There are many different ways to layout the Visual Basic IDE, and different versions of Visual Basic and Visual Studio have different features. That means the illustrations in this book may not look exactly the same as what appears on your screen. However, the steps given here will apply whatever layout you use.

There is an option to run the IDE in "Tabbed Document" or "MDI" mode. Tabbed Document is preferred and is the default, but you might want to experiment. You can also reset the window layout to the default, if it gets untidy. These options are in Tools > Options > Environment > General.

Menu bar   Toolbars   Tabbed work area   Docked tool window   Auto-hidden window

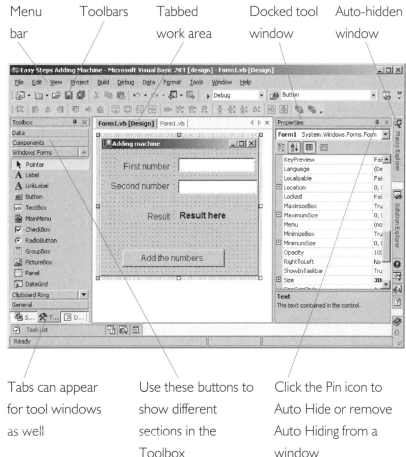

Tabs can appear for tool windows as well

Use these buttons to show different sections in the Toolbox

Click the Pin icon to Auto Hide or remove Auto Hiding from a window

Your first application

To get started with Visual Basic, here is how to create an application in four easy steps:

The secret of VB is using events, properties and methods to bring your forms to life. This chapter begins to show you how to do this, using step-by-step examples.

1 Start Visual Basic or Visual Studio and click the New Project icon, or choose New Project from the File menu.

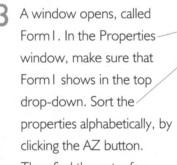

2 In the New Project dialog click on Windows Application. Then type FirstApp in the Name box. Next, click OK to start the project.

If you cannot find the Properties window, or any of the other main Visual Basic windows, choose it from the View menu. Then it will pop back into view. You can also press F4 to show the Properties window.

3 A window opens, called Form1. In the Properties window, make sure that Form1 shows in the top drop-down. Sort the properties alphabetically, by clicking the AZ button. Then find the entry for Text, and type over Form1 so it says Easy Steps.

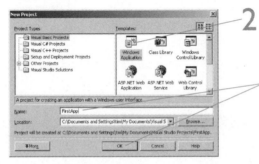

In this book, the illustrations show the Properties window sorted alphabetically. If you prefer, you can sort by categories, but the list will then be in a different order from the illustrations.

4 In the Toolbar, click the Start button (small right arrow) to run. This first application just creates a window. It is a proper one. You can resize, move or minimise it, and finally quit the application by closing it. It may not do much but you've just created a Windows program!

First look at the Toolbox

Visual Basic's Toolbox contains the building bricks of your applications. Using the form from the previous page, follow these steps to try it now:

While you work in Visual Basic, the Pointer icon will be selected most of the time. Only select the other icons in the Toolbox when you want to place a new object on a form.

| Click the "A" icon on the Toolbox. This is the icon for a label. It will change appearance to show it is depressed.

The exact contents of the Toolbox vary according to which version of Visual Basic you have and how you have set it up. If you right-click the Toolbox, you will see a menu that lets you add and remove the Toolbox components.

2 Move the mouse pointer over the form, and press down the left mouse button where you want to position the top-left corner of the label. Keep it pressed down as you drag the mouse down and right to enlarge the label. Then release the button. If it is not quite right, you can move it with the mouse, or resize it using one of the eight resize tabs.

Resize tabs

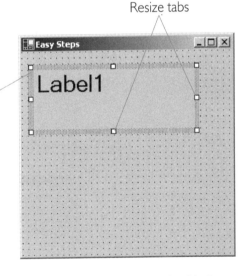

First look at the Property Editor

Visual Basic's Property Editor is a list of characteristics. Each characteristic or "property" affects the currently selected object, such as a label or button, on a form. By changing these properties, you control the appearance of the object.

Changing the properties of a label

1 Drag a label from the Toolbox onto a form. You can use the example from the previous page if you like. Make sure the label is selected.

Every object in Visual Basic has a name. At the top of the Properties window, the name of the currently selected object is shown.

2 Now click in the right-hand column of the Properties window to change some values:

- Change BorderStyle to "Fixed Single"
- Change Text to "My custom label"
- Change TextAlign to "TopCenter" (click on the centre block in the drop-down image)

Notice how the appearance of the label alters to reflect your changes

Getting to know Visual Basic forms

Most Visual Basic applications are based on a form. The form is a canvas on which you paint your application. In many cases, there will be more than one form, and Visual Basic lets you display and hide forms while the application is running. Closing the main form quits the application.

A form is a window. That is why forms have Minimize, Maximize and Close buttons, just like other kinds of window.

Like all Visual Basic objects, forms have properties. To select a form, so that its properties appear in the Properties window, click anywhere on the background of a form.

Key form properties

Icon: small picture that appears at top-left or when the form is minimised

Text: words that appears in the title bar of the form

This is the Text

FormBorderStyle: determines what the form's edges look like; if you can resize it with the mouse; and which buttons appear at top-right. This example is set to Sizeable

BackColor: determines the background colour of the form

StartPosition: controls the position at which the form first appears on the Windows desktop

Placing a Visual Basic button

A button is one of Visual Basic's most useful objects. Buttons put the user in control of your application. Using Visual Basic, you determine what happens when the user clicks the button with the mouse.

Placing a button on a form

To make the illustration easier to read, I have increased the font size for the label and the button. To do this, edit the Font property in the Properties window. If you click the + symbol to the left of the Font property, this shows sub-properties including the Size, which you can then change.

I Click the Button icon in the Toolbox so that it is depressed.

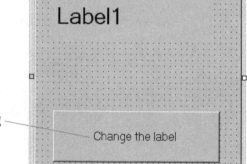

2 Click on the form, drag down and right, and release the mouse to place a button. You can resize the button with the resize tabs or move it by clicking on the button, holding down the left mouse button and then dragging.

When you type text for a button, menu or other control, the & character has a special meaning. The & does not display. Instead, the following character is underlined. By pressing the Alt key in combination with the underlined character, the object can be clicked without using the mouse. This is called a keyboard shortcut.

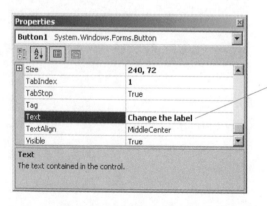

3 Use the Properties window to make the button's Text "Change the label".

First look at Visual Basic events

Most Windows software works by responding to the actions of the user. For example, when you press a key in a word-processor, a character appears in a document. An event (pressing a key) is followed by a response (the document is updated).

This process of responding to events is vital for creating Visual Basic applications. You write instructions to be carried out when a particular event takes place. A classic example is the clicking of a button.

You do not have to double-click to open the code editor. Instead, you can right-click an object and choose View Code from the pop-up menu that appears.

To see how this works, place a button on a form, or use the example from the previous page. Now double-click the button with the mouse. Visual Basic opens a text editor, with some text already entered. It looks like this:

```
Private Sub Button1_Click()
End Sub
```

It is between these two lines that you will write code that will run when the button gets clicked.

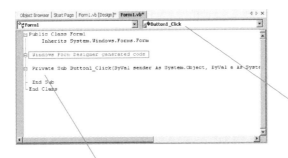

Buttons can respond to other events as well. To see all the events, select Button 1 in the left-hand drop-down, and then drop-down the right-hand list

Double-click a button to open the code editor, ready for you to type in your code. To get started, this is where you type, between the Private Sub and End Sub lines

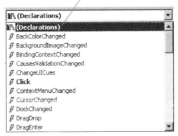

Your first line of code

To try this example, you need a form with a button and a label.

1 Open the code editor for Click events by double-clicking the button.

2 Type "Label1." (not forgetting the dot). A drop-down menu appears. Type "t" and the list jumps to the T section. Use the down arrow to move to Text so it is highlighted. Press the Spacebar, and the word "Text" is automatically entered.

The coding feature used here is called Auto List Members. Although it is handy, some people find it annoying. If so, you can switch it off using the Options dialog, available from the Tools menu. In the Options dialog, you need to find the Tab for Text Editor > Basic > Auto List Members.

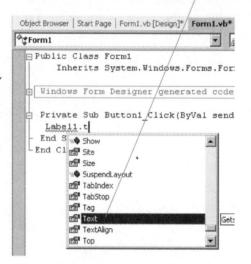

3 Complete the line of code by typing so it reads:

```
Label1.Text =
"I've been
changed"
```

You can also select a property in an Auto List Members list by double-clicking on the property you want.

4 Run the application by clicking the Start button on Visual Basic's toolbar. Now click the button. The label's caption changes.

Setting properties in code

Let's look a little closer at the code you wrote for the button's Click event. Here it is again:

```
Label1.Text = "I've been changed"
```

Now, you could have created a label with this caption another way. If you selected the label, and typed into the Text property in the Properties window, that would have the same result.

The example on this page shows how you can set properties for alignment and colour. These properties are really numbers, but to make them easier to remember you can use constants like Color.Yellow instead. Auto List Members shows what constants are available.

The code you wrote tells Visual Basic to set the Text property of the object called Label1 to the value "I've been changed".

The advantage of setting property values in code is that you don't need to know beforehand what the values will be. You can determine them at run-time. You can see this working in the next application.

In the meantime, try setting some more label properties in code to see how effective this can be:

Type in and run this example to show how you can set the properties of a Visual Basic object in code. Use Auto List Members to save typing long expressions like ContentAlignment.MiddleCenter

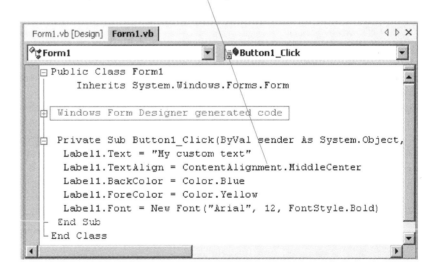

A Visual Basic adding machine

This example is more interesting, in that it performs a useful function. It adds two numbers and displays the result. It introduces a new object, the TextBox.

Creating the adding machine

If you need to refer to an object in your code, it is a good idea to give it a meaningful name. For example, lbResult contains a prefix, lb, to remind you that it is a label. The second part, Result, describes what it is for.

1 This is a TextBox in the Toolbox window.

Add two of them to a form and set the Text property to nothing.

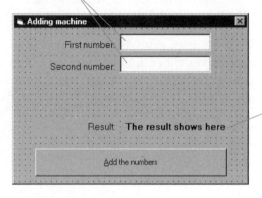

2 Next add four labels and a button as shown.

3 Set this label's name property to lbResult using the Properties window (see page 14 for an example).

When typing Visual Basic code, you don't usually have to worry about capitals or lower case letters. Visual Basic is not case-sensitive. Even so, code is easier to read if you are consistent and always use capitals in the same way.

4 There is just one line of code for the button's Click event:

```
LbResult.Text = Str(Val(TextBox1.Text) +
Val(TextBox2.Text))
```

Don't worry if the code looks puzzling – it's explained in Chapter Three.

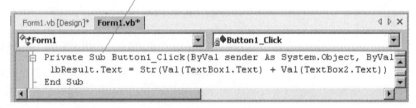

5 Now test the application by clicking the Start button. Type a number in each of the TextBoxes, and click the button to add the two together and show the result.

Dealing with errors

We all make mistakes. What happens if you try to run an application that contains typing errors or faulty code? For example, what if you typed `TextBox1.Txt` instead of `TextBox1.Text`? In most cases, Visual Basic will halt and display an error message. Then it will show the line of code which caused the error.

Visual Basic stops and displays an error message:

If you click on an error in the Task List, and then press F1, Visual Basic will often display a detailed Help entry that explains more about the error and how to fix it.

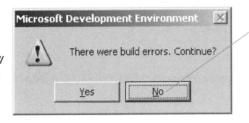

2 Click No. Then look at the Task List which pops up with a list of errors.

3 Double-click an error in the Task List to jump to that point in the code.

You can write code to catch errors and make your programs more robust. This is introduced in Chapter Eight.

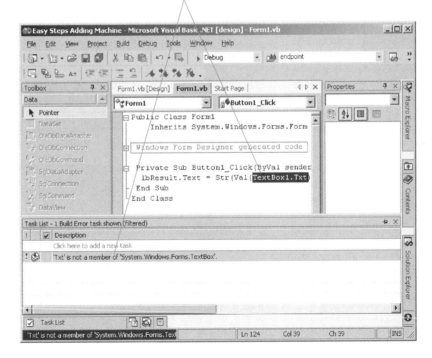

How to get Help

Although it makes programming as simple as possible, there's a lot to remember in Visual Basic and some operations are complex. It is important to learn how to use the on-line Help.

Help through ToolTips

Because Visual Basic is very popular, there are lots of other sources of assistance, including books, magazines and discussions on the Internet.

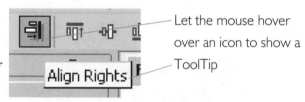

Let the mouse hover over an icon to show a ToolTip

Help through Visual Basic Help

You can also get help from MSDN ("Microsoft Developer Network"). From the Help menu, choose Contents to open the online version of Visual Basic's manuals and other manuals and articles.

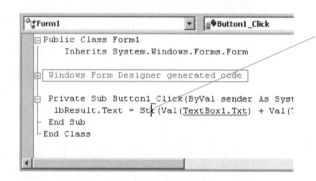

1 Place the cursor in the word for which you want help.

MSDN contains a huge amount of information. Set "Filtered by" to Visual Basic to find the key Visual Basic entries quickly. If it is slow, run Setup again and choose to copy more of MSDN to your hard disk for better performance, provided of course you have plenty of free disk space.

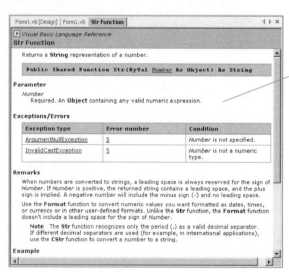

2 Press F1 to bring up help on that particular word, if available.

Searching Help

This is a short book but even a long one can't contain all the detail in online Help. The problem is finding the right entry. It is hard because the MSDN library (online Help) supplied with Visual Basic covers many languages and topics (including C++ and other languages). Here are some tips on finding the right information:

How to search Help

When you search online Help, try to narrow down the search by including several words. You can use quotation marks to search for an expression of more than one word, such as "Visual Basic", as well as the AND, OR, NOT operators. You can also set a filter. Here is an example:

Along with search, there is also a Help index (Help > Index). Use this with filters for the best results. If you want help on a Visual Basic keyword, placing the cursor on the word in the editor and pressing F1 is often the quickest way to find it.

Imagine you want help on the Image property of a PictureBox. From the Help menu, choose Search or press Ctrl+Alt+F3. Type words into the search box. If you just type "Image Property", the maximum 500 topics are returned, most of little relevance

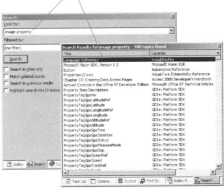

Setting a filter is a lengthy operation. However, once set, it performs well until you change it.

If you add a filter for "Visual Basic and Related", it narrows to just 32 topics. Double-click an entry to show the document. Click here to set a filter

When you search for several words, the AND operator is implied by default. Use OR if you want the maximum number of results.

If you type "Image Property PictureBox Visual Basic" you find just 58 topics, many of which are relevant

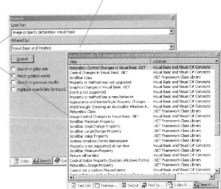

First look at the Solution Explorer

A Visual Basic application can contain more than one form. It can also include modules of pure code, not attached to any form, and several other more advanced elements. Managing the items in a large project can get difficult. The Solution Explorer is a window which lists all the items in your project. If the Solution Explorer is not visible, select it from the View menu or press Ctrl+Alt+l.

If you can't see the Solution Explorer, Properties Window, Toolbox, or other Visual Basic windows, then you can use the View menu to bring them back.

Click here to view the code editor for the selected object

Click here to view the object itself, for example a form

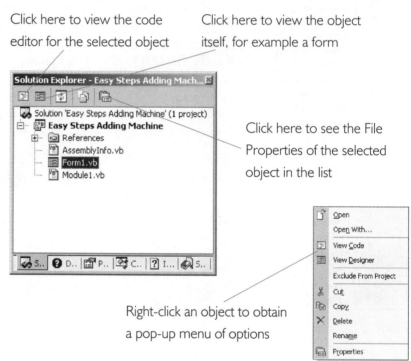

Click here to see the File Properties of the selected object in the list

Right-click an object to obtain a pop-up menu of options

When to use the Solution Explorer

Use the Solution Explorer when you want to view an object such as a form or code module. These are not always visible, even when a project is loaded. By using the Solution Explorer you can keep an uncluttered screen, just viewing the particular objects you are working on.

If you have a large project, the Solution Explorer is essential for finding the form or code which you need to work on next. You can also open several related projects at once, which is why it is called the Solution Explorer instead of the Project Explorer.

Saving your project

Visual Basic always creates a new folder (directory) for a Visual Basic project. This makes it easy to manage your work — for example, moving, deleting or backing-up the project.

A Visual Basic project consists of more than one file when saved to disk. For example, the simplest Windows Form project contains a project file, with the extension .vbproj, a form file, with the extension .vb, and a number of other files.

When you chose Save from the File menu only the file currently active is saved. To save an entire project, choose Save All. If you close Visual Basic you will be prompted to save any unsaved files.

The name of a file is determined by the name you choose when adding a new item, such as a form or module. To change the file name, select it in the Solution Explorer and choose Properties. Note that the File Properties are different from the regular Properties for an object.

How to change the file name of a form

If you want to change the name of a file in a project, it is best to do this from the Solution Explorer rather than searching out the file on disk and renaming it directly. Otherwise, Visual Basic will think the file is missing next time you open the project.

On the other hand, If you want to make a copy of an entire project, simply copy the directory from outside Visual Basic, and open the copy you have made.

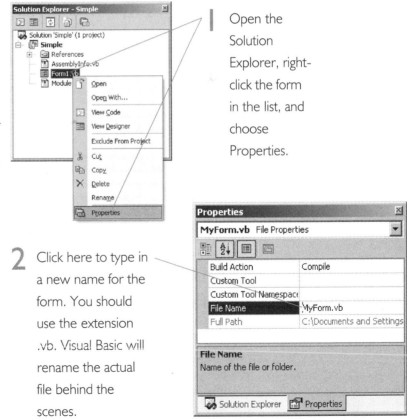

Open the Solution Explorer, right-click the form in the list, and choose Properties.

2 Click here to type in a new name for the form. You should use the extension .vb. Visual Basic will rename the actual file behind the scenes.

Reopening an application

To reopen a Visual Basic project, use the following steps:

1 Choose Open > Project from the File menu.

Visual Basic also lets you open projects and solutions through File > Recent Projects, and through the Start Page which lists the projects you have been working on.

2 Find the project file (with a .vproj extension) or the solution (with a .sln extension) and click on it to highlight it.

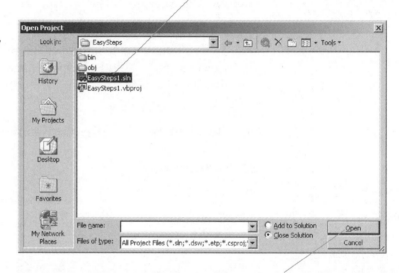

3 Click Open.

Having more than one project open can be confusing. It's best to open just one project at a time, except when you absolutely need several open together, for example for advanced component programming.

Opening more than one project at once

Visual Basic lets you open more than one project at once. To do this, select Add to Solution when you open a project. It will be added to the projects already open in Visual Basic.

Project or solution?

A solution is a container for one or more projects. If you open a solution, all the projects it contains will be opened. When the solution contains a single project, it often makes little difference whether you open the solution or the project it contains. However, solutions can contain files and settings that are outside any project, so it is normally preferable to work with the solution.

Controls Explained

Visual Basic gives you a wide range of pre-defined objects which you can use to assemble an application. This chapter describes each of the key objects in the Visual Basic Toolbox.

Covers

Chapter Two

Controls and methods

The objects in the Visual Basic Toolbox are often called controls. Most of the controls represent things that will be familiar to you if you have worked with other Windows applications.

We saw in Chapter One that controls have properties which determine their appearance and how they work. Controls also have events, actions that trigger a response. Before looking more closely at individual examples, there is another feature of Visual Basic controls with which you need to be familiar – the concept of methods.

What is a method?

If you look up a control in Visual Basic Help, you will see that Properties, Events and Methods are listed. Together, these tell you almost everything about what the control can do. The easiest way to find the help entry is to click on the button with the mouse so it is selected, and then press F1.

A property is something an object *has*. By contrast, a method is something that it *does*.

For example, a motor vehicle has properties, like colour, model, age and speed. But what about starting and stopping? These are things that a vehicle does. If a vehicle were a Visual Basic object, Start and Stop would be two of its methods. Often, methods have extra information called parameters. These appear in brackets after the method name, and specify how the action is to take place. For example, a vehicle might stop quickly or slowly. Even when there are no parameters, you still need to include the brackets.

An example

Labels have a Hide method which makes them invisible, and a Show method that makes them visible.

You could put a second button on the form that runs Label1.Show(), in order to show the label again. Hiding and showing objects is a handy technique to learn.

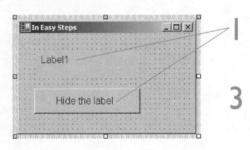

1 Place a label and a button on a form.

3 Run the application and click the button.

2 In the button's Click event, type:

`Label1.Hide()`

Using buttons

Too many buttons on a form are confusing for the user. Consider using additional forms or a tabbed dialog instead.

If you have worked through Chapter One, you will already be familiar with buttons. Use buttons when you want an easy way for users to kick off an operation, confirm or cancel a choice, or get help.

Most of your work with buttons involves setting properties and writing code for one event, Click.

If you want a button to Click when the user presses Return, set the form's **AcceptButton** *property to the name of the button. If you want another button to Click when Escape is pressed, set the* **CancelButton** *property to the name of that button.*

The Text property determines what text appears on the button. Use the & character to create a keyboard shortcut

Use the sizing tabs to resize the button

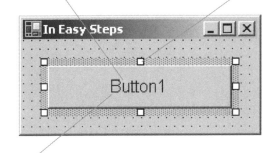

The Font property lets you change the font used for the caption

For a more interesting appearance, set the Image property to an image. Then set the ImageAlign property to TopCenter and TextAlign to BottomCenter. Make the button high enough to show both elements. You can even specify a list of images so that you can change them in code when the button is down or disabled

The Enabled and Disabled properties are usually set in the code, to prevent a button from being clicked at the wrong time.

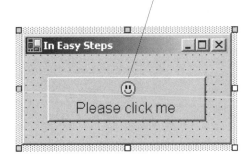

Using labels

The label control is another Visual Basic object you will be familiar with from Chapter One. Use labels to display text that the user does not need to edit. You can still change the text displayed in your code, by setting the Text property.

You can include an image in a label by setting the Image and ImageAlign properties

A white or coloured background creates a more striking appearance

You can get some great effects by setting a label's BackColor property to Transparent. Then you can superimpose text on a picture or other background graphics.

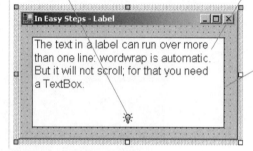

Set the BorderStyle property to FixedSingle for this boxed effect

How to align labels

There is also a Make Same Size option on the Format menu. This works like the Align option, but adjusts the size of the labels. Using both, you can soon have neat-looking labels. These techniques also work with other controls.

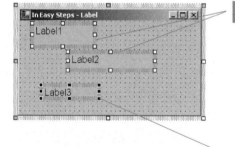

1 Place several labels on a form. Select all the ones you need to align by holding Shift down as you click on each in turn. The last one you select will be the master, to which the others align. Note the darker sizing tabs on this label.

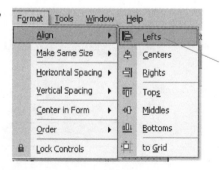

2 Choose Align from the Format menu. Choose Lefts from the submenu to align the labels to the left edge of the master.

Using TextBoxes

TextBoxes are an essential part of most Visual Basic applications. The key difference between a label and a TextBox is that you can type into a TextBox at runtime. Another difference is that TextBoxes can display large amounts of text which the user can scroll through. TextBoxes were used in the Adding Machine application described in Chapter One.

Creating a scrollable TextBox

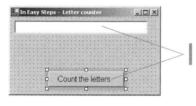

To create a scrollable TextBox, set its Multiline property to True and its Scrollbars property to Vertical

A letter-counting application

This example shows how to access a TextBox in code.

If you have a long line of Basic code, you may want to break it into several lines. If you type a space followed by an underline character at the end of a line, Visual Basic considers the following line to be part of the same statement.

Place a TextBox and a button on a form.

2 Add this code to the button's Click event:

```
MsgBox ("You typed: " & _
Str(Len(TextBox1.Text)) & " characters")
```

3 Test the application by running it, entering some text in the TextBox, and clicking the button.

Using PictureBoxes

A PictureBox, as its name suggests, is a box which can contain a picture. Less obviously, you can draw on a PictureBox in your code. A PictureBox can also be a container for other controls, so you can group them together.

Not all picture files can be loaded directly into a PictureBox. In addition, there are many variations on even standard formats like .bmp or .wmf. If necessary, you can use additional software to convert pictures from one format to another.

Loading a picture

1 Click the PictureBox icon in the Toolbox and place one on a form. Make sure it is selected.

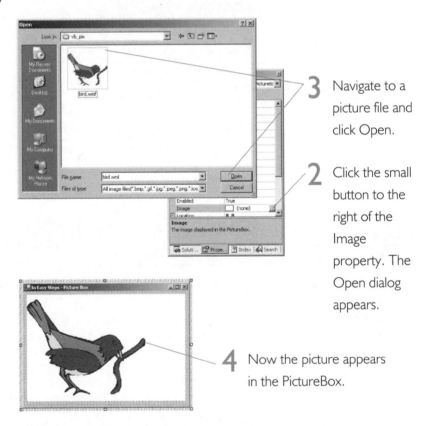

3 Navigate to a picture file and click Open.

2 Click the small button to the right of the Image property. The Open dialog appears.

4 Now the picture appears in the PictureBox.

Which pictures can I load?

You can load bitmaps, icons and metafiles. Bitmaps must have a BMP, JPG, JPEG, GIF or PNG extension. Icons have an ICO extension. Metafiles have either a WMF or EMF extension. The advantage of metafiles is that you can scale the picture larger or smaller without loss of quality.

Using CheckBoxes

A CheckBox is a small box with a caption. When the user clicks the box, a check mark appears. Another click removes the mark.

CheckBoxes are ideal when you want to present a set of options from which the user can choose none, one or more than one. In the example which follows, a pizza restaurant has a form for specifying which extra toppings the customer would like.

If you have a set of options where the user may only choose one, use a RadioButton instead of a CheckBox.

The Pizza application

1 Click the CheckBox icon in the Toolbox and place three on a form.

2 Add a label and button, setting the Text properties to some tempting pizza toppings. Name the CheckBoxes, for example chkMushrooms, chkHam and chkHot.

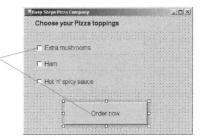

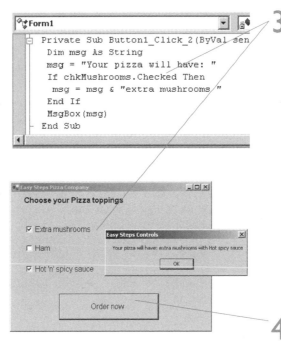

It doesn't matter if you can't yet follow the code in an application like this. Visual Basic code is tackled in the next chapter. For now, you only need to know what a CheckBox is for.

3 You can write code to find whether a box is checked by inspecting its Checked property. If it is True, then it is checked. This code is just the start, and only looks at the first CheckBox.

4 Enjoy your pizza!

Using RadioButtons

A RadioButton is like a CheckBox, but with one important difference: you can only have one button in a group checked. Checking a RadioButton automatically unchecks any others. For example, a pizza can be thin-crust or deep-pan, but not both.

Thin-crust or deep-pan?

When you lay out a group of option buttons, set the Checked property of one of them to True. Otherwise, when the application runs they will all be unchecked.

1 Click the RadioButton icon in the Toolbox and place two on a form.

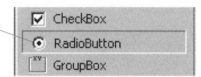

2 Add a label and a button and set the Text properties as shown. Name the buttons rbThin and rbDeep. Choose one of the RadioButtons and set the Checked property to True.

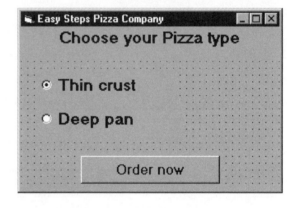

You could combine this application with the previous one, so that the user could choose toppings and pizza type from the same form.

3 Write code to inspect the Checked property of the RadioButtons. If it is True, then it is checked.

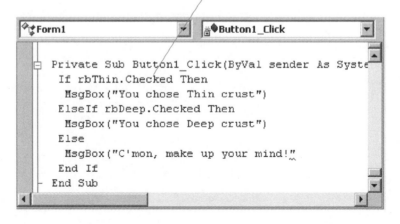

```
Form1                          Button1_Click

  Private Sub Button1_Click(ByVal sender As Syste
    If rbThin.Checked Then
      MsgBox("You chose Thin crust")
    ElseIf rbDeep.Checked Then
      MsgBox("You chose Deep crust")
    Else
      MsgBox("C'mon, make up your mind!")
    End If
  End Sub
```

Using GroupBoxes

A GroupBox is a container for other objects. It is particularly useful for grouping objects that work together, like RadioButtons.

Pizzas in the box

You can check whether a control is in a GroupBox by moving the GroupBox. Controls that are in the GroupBox will move with it.

1 Click the GroupBox icon in the Toolbox and place two on a form.

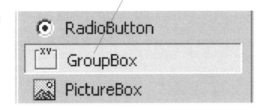

2 Set the Text property for each GroupBox to describe its options.

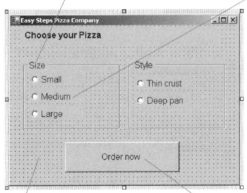

If you want two objects to match, like the GroupBoxes in this example, select them both together using Shift-click, and then use the Align and Make Same Size options.

3 Click the RadioButton icon in the Toolbox and place buttons on each GroupBox. When placing the buttons, be sure your first click is on the GroupBox. Otherwise, the RadioButton will be on the form and not the GroupBox.

4 Try running the application and notice how the two groups of RadioButtons work independently.

5 You can write code for the Click event of this button to detect the choices made, by looking at the Checked property of each RadioButton.

Using ListBoxes

The ListBox is one of the most useful and powerful Visual Basic controls. When you want to present choices to the user, a list is more flexible than a row of CheckBoxes or RadioButtons, because the number of items in the list can vary from one or two to many thousands. Databases like address books or business records often use lists to present the information.

Adding items to a ListBox

This is the first use in this book of a form's Load event. The Load event is ideal for placing code that runs before the user sees the form.

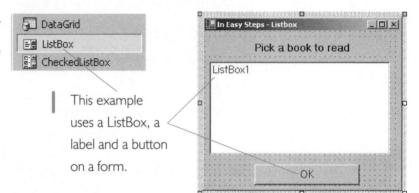

This example uses a ListBox, a label and a button on a form.

You can also fill a ListBox from the Properties window. The ListBox has an Items collection, and if you click this you can type entries directly into the list. It is usually more useful to fill the ListBox from code.

2 Set the ListBox's Sorted property to True, so that items in the list will be sorted alphabetically.

3 Double-click the form to open its Load event. Use the ListBox.Items.Add method to add items to the ListBox. For example:

```
ListBox1.Items.Add("Visual
Basic .Net in easy steps")
```

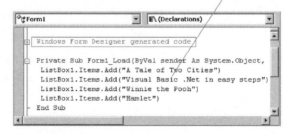

4 Run the application to see the ListBox filled.

ListBoxes are not restricted to storing strings. You can store almost any kind of object in a ListBox. The displayed value is that returned by the object's ToString() method.

It is no use adding items to a list unless you can tell which one the user has picked. There are two ways to do so. At runtime, the ListIndex property tells you which row in the list is selected, usually by the user clicking on that row. The Text property tells you the text in the selected row. If no row is selected, the ListIndex property is -1.

Retrieving an item from a ListBox

1 Your code should first check the SelectedIndex property. If it is -1, nothing is selected. If it is anything other than -1, use the Text property to find the contents of the chosen row.

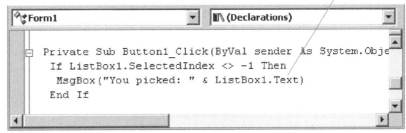

```
Form1                          (Declarations)

  Private Sub Button1_Click(ByVal sender As System.Obje
    If ListBox1.SelectedIndex <> -1 Then
      MsgBox("You picked: " & ListBox1.Text)
    End If
```

If you wanted an item in the ListBox to be already selected when the form opens, you could set the SelectedIndex property in the Form Load event, like this:

`ListBox1.SelectedIndex = 0`

(Note that the first item in the list is 0, not 1.)

2 Now run the application. If nothing is selected in the ListBox and you click OK, nothing happens. If a book title is selected, it appears in a message box when you click OK.

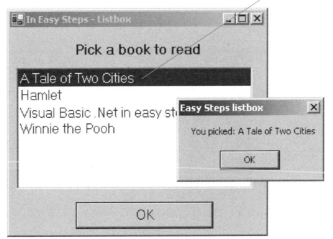

Using CheckedListBoxes

A CheckedListBox is an enhanced ListBox that lets you check and uncheck items in the list.

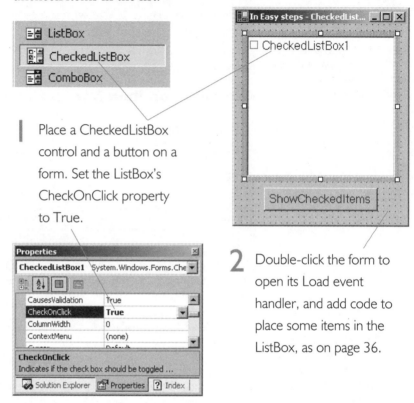

Place a CheckedListBox control and a button on a form. Set the ListBox's CheckOnClick property to True.

2 Double-click the form to open its Load event handler, and add code to place some items in the ListBox, as on page 36.

3 Double-click the button to open its Click event handler, and type this code, to display the checked items.

This code only works because the items stored in the ListBox are of type String. If the objects are of a different type, you would need to use the corresponding type for the item variable.

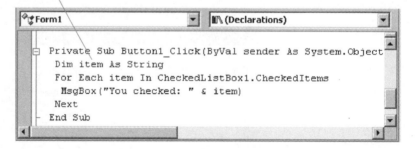

```
Private Sub Button1_Click(ByVal sender As System.Object
   Dim item As String
   For Each item In CheckedListBox1.CheckedItems
     MsgBox("You checked: " & item)
   Next
 End Sub
```

4 Run the application, check some items, and then click the button. The checked items are displayed one by one.

Using ComboBoxes

A ComboBox is a one-line TextBox combined with a ListBox. The advantage over a normal TextBox is that the most common choices can be presented without any need to type them in. The advantage over a ListBox is that a ComboBox takes less space. ComboBoxes also allow the user to type in a choice that is not on the list. The example here is a person's title. Usually this is one of a few common options: Mr, Mrs, Miss etc. The range of possibilities though is much greater, including rarities like Princess or President. The ComboBox is an ideal solution.

Placing a ComboBox

You can retrieve the value the user has chosen by inspecting the Text property of the ComboBox.

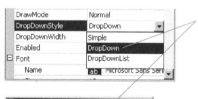

1 Place a ComboBox on a form. The other labels and TextBoxes on the form shown are not essential to run the example.

2 Open the Load event for the form and write code to fill the ComboBox, for example:

```
Combo1.AddItem ("Mr")
Combo1.AddItem ("Mrs")
```

If you don't want the user choosing a value not on the list, choose DropDownList.

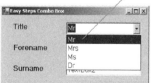

3 Try setting the DropDownStyle property to different values and then running the application. Dropdown is the default.

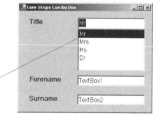

4 To use Simple Combo you need to increase the height of the ComboBox.

The OpenFileDialog Control

Many Windows applications need to load or save files on disk. That could involve writing a lot of code, but fortunately Visual Basic makes it easy to use the standard Windows dialog for this.

Controls like OpenFileDialog and SaveFileDialog are similar to other controls, in that you use them by selecting an icon in the Toolbox and placing it on a form. They are different, though, because they appear in a space below the form in the Designer, and are invisible when the application runs. However you can refer to them in code.

Creating a Picture Viewer

When you run the Picture Viewer, you will find that images may be too small or too large to fill the control properly. If you set the SizeMode property to StretchImage, it will be stretched to exactly fill the control. This will also distort the picture, so use it with care. Another option is CenterImage.

1 Place a PictureBox, a button, and an OpenFileDialog Control on a form.

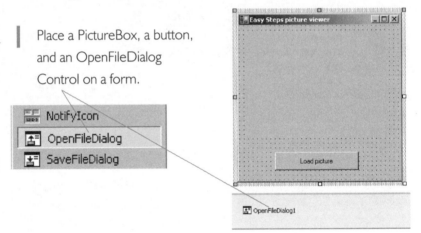

Often you have a choice between setting a property in the Properties window, or in the Load event for a form. It doesn't matter which you choose. It is easier to type longer properties into the Load event, instead of the small boxes of the Properties window. It also makes it easier to find and edit the code, which is rather hidden away when in the Properties window.

2 Open the form's Load event and add the line:

```
OpenFileDialog1.Filter = _
"Pictures|*.bmp;*.ico;*.jpg;*.wmf"
```

Then add the following lines to the button's Click event:

```
OpenFileDialog1.ShowDialog()
If OpenFileDialog1.FileName <> "" Then
  PictureBox1.Image = New
Bitmap(OpenFileDialog1.FileName)
End If
```

Now you can test the application by running it, clicking the button, and finding a bitmap file in the dialog.

...cont'd

There is a group of controls that work in a similar way.
Once you understand how the OpenFileDialog Control works, it is easy to use the other dialogs like SaveFileDialog and FontDialog.

The exact appearance of this dialog will vary according to the version of Windows being used. Images may appear as lines in a list, rather than previews as here.

The Picture Viewer works, but if the user chooses a file that is not a picture, it crashes with an error message. See Chapter Eight for how to handle such errors.

More about the OpenFileDialog control

The OpenFileDialog saves the programmer from writing a lot of code to correctly navigate a hard disk or network and find or create files. The Picture Viewer example uses ShowDialog to summon the standard Windows Open dialog.

When it opens, the dialog uses the Filter property to decide which files to show. This helps prevent the user from trying to open the wrong sort of file for your application. When the user clicks Open, the dialog disappears and the name of the chosen file is placed in the Filename property of the OpenFileDialog Control.

The title of the dialog is set by the DialogTitle property

The Filter property sets what appears here. This property has two or more parts, separated by the | character. The first is what shows in the 'Files of type:' box. The second lists acceptable extensions, divided by a semi-colon

If the user clicks Cancel, the Filename property will be empty

Using the timer

The timer is an invisible control like the OpenFileDialog. All it does is to fire an event at intervals set by you.

You can change the interval property of a timer at runtime. In this example, you could have an option to slow down the flashing or speed it up. You can also move the lights by changing the Top and Left properties of the label control.

Make the lights flash!

The following example uses two labels, and makes them flash alternately blue and yellow. Controlling the flash is a Visual Basic Timer control, which is an essential part of many animation effects.

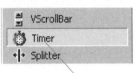

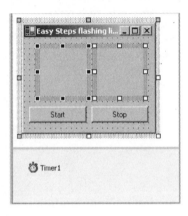

1 Place a timer, two labels and two buttons on a form. Set the timer's Interval property to 200. This time is in milliseconds. Set one label's BackColor property to Blue, and the other to Yellow.

2 Double-click the timer to open the Tick event. This will run every time the interval elapses. Add this code:

```
Static toggle As Boolean
If toggle = True Then
  Label1.BackColor = Color.Blue
  Label2.BackColor = Color.Yellow
Else
  Label1.BackColor = Color.Yellow
  Label2.BackColor = Color.Blue
End If
toggle = Not toggle
```

The timer is not as accurate as it first appears. Although the interval is specified in milliseconds, the resolution of the timer is probably 50 times worse than that.

3 For the Start Button's Click event add:

```
Timer1.Enabled = True
```

The Stop Button is the same, but with False.

4 Run the application and see the lights flash!

Using the Tab control

When designing Visual Basic forms, it is easy to run out of space. The Tab control lets you separate groups of controls into different tabs, increasing the space available without much inconvenience to the user.

An example

1 Place a Tab control on a form. Set its Dock property to Fill. Then click the small button next to TabPages (Collection), to open the TabPage editor.

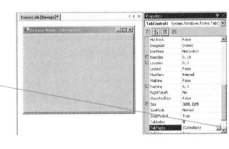

Once the tabs have been added, you can edit their properties from the form itself, without going back to the TabPage editor. You can also use Add Tab and Remove Tab buttons that appear at the foot of the Properties window when a TabControl is selected.

2 In the TabPage editor, click Add twice, to add two TabPages. Then click OK.

If you place controls on the form, behind the Tab control, they will be visible on all the TabPages. In order to place controls on the form, you will need to temporarily undock the Tab control and move it out of the way.

3 Next, simply layout the form in the normal way, clicking the TabPage tabs to bring the required section to the front.

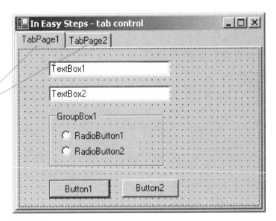

Using the Splitter control

The Splitter control allows the user to resize controls relative to one another at runtime.

An example

Place a ListBox control on a form. Set its Dock property to Left. Next, place a Splitter control on the form, and set its Dock property to Left. Finally, place a TextBox control, set its MultiLine property to True and its Dock property to Fill.

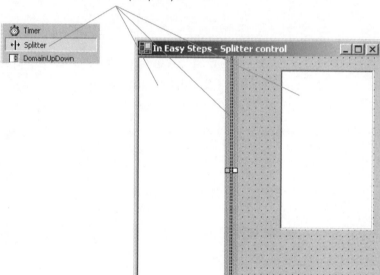

Make sure you add and dock the controls in the right order. If the Splitter is docked right to the edge of the form, instead of on the edge of a control, it will not work.

If you dock the Splitter control to the Top or Bottom, then it becomes a horizontal bar.

Run the application, and test the Splitter by clicking on it with the mouse and dragging to left or right. In this example, some items have also been added to the list, and some text to the TextBox.

Using the Toolbar and RichTextBox

The RichTextBox is a more powerful version of the TextBox, able to display and edit formatted text. The Toolbar is a row of buttons grouped together on a bar. This example uses both to create a simple word processor.

If you find the RichTextBox going behind the toolbar when you set Dock to fill, try deleting the RichTextBox and adding it back. This can sometimes fix problems with the docking.

1 Place a Toolbar, a RichTextBox and a FontDialogBox on a form. Set the RichTextBox's Dock property to Fill. Set its Font property to a font of your choice.

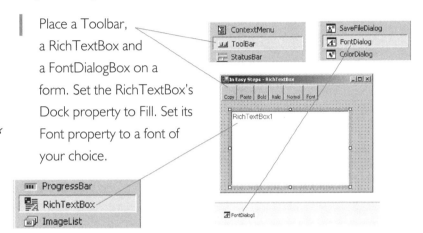

2 Click on the Toolbar, then click the small button in the Properties window to open the Buttons collection. Click Add six times. Set the button Text to Copy, Paste, Bold, Italic, Normal and Font.

3 Double-click a Toolbar button to open its Click event. Toolbar buttons share one Click event handler. You can detect which button was clicked by inspecting the ToolBarButtonClickEventArgs argument. This argument has a Button property that references the ToolBarButton that was actually clicked. See the next page for a Select Case statement that determines which button was clicked and runs the appropriate code.

This is not a complete word processor, but it gives an idea of what you can do. The native format of the RichTextBox is RTF, which is a standard format used by most word processors and also by the Windows clipboard. By adding an OpenFileDialog and a SaveFileDialog you can easily add the capability to load and save documents from disk.

One thing you cannot easily do with the RichTextBox control, in the first version of Visual Basic .Net, is to print. If you search out Visual Basic resources on the Internet, you can find code for printing a RichTextBox.

4 Add this code to the Toolbar's Click event handler:

```
'Get a valid font
Dim f As Font
f = RichTextBox1.SelectionFont
If f Is Nothing Then
 f = RichTextBox1.Font
End If

'Take action depending on the text on the Button
Select Case e.Button.Text
 Case "Copy"
  RichTextBox1.Copy()
 Case "Paste"
  RichTextBox1.Paste()
 Case "Bold"
  RichTextBox1.SelectionFont = _
  New Font(f, FontStyle.Bold)
 Case "Italic"
  RichTextBox1.SelectionFont = _
  New Font(f, FontStyle.Italic)
 Case "Normal"
  RichTextBox1.SelectionFont = _
  New Font(f, FontStyle.Regular)
 Case "Font"
  If FontDialog1.ShowDialog() = _
  DialogResult.OK Then
   RichTextBox1.SelectionFont = FontDialog1.Font
  End If
End Select
```

5 Run the application. To make text bold or italic, select it and press the Bold or Italic button. You can also Copy and Paste, even with images.

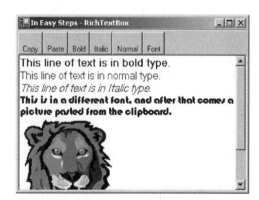

Using the MonthCalendar control

Many Visual Basic applications deal with dates. Two controls make it easy to select and display dates. The MonthCalendar displays a month to view, with buttons for moving to other months. The DateTimePicker is a drop-down MonthCalendar, ideal for saving space on forms where you need to display a single date. The MonthCalendar lets you select a range of dates. You can retrieve the start date from the SelectionStart property, and the end date from the SelectionEnd property.

1 Place a MonthCalendar and a TextBox on a form. Set the TextBox's Multiline property to True, and Dock to Bottom.

2 Double-click the MonthCalendar to open its DateChanged event handler. Add this code:

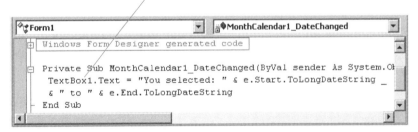

```
Form1                              MonthCalendar1_DateChanged

  Windows Form Designer generated code

  Private Sub MonthCalendar1_DateChanged(ByVal sender As System.Ob
    TextBox1.Text = "You selected: " & e.Start.ToLongDateString _
    & " to " & e.End.ToLongDateString
  End Sub
```

3 Run the application, and select a range of dates to try it out. Click the month name to drop-down a list of months. The dates selected appear in the TextBox.

Setting tab order

It is important to realise that not all users like to use the mouse. Therefore you should allow keyboard alternatives wherever possible. One way is by keyboard shortcuts for buttons and menu options. Another factor is that users expect to be able to move the focus from one control to another by pressing Tab. You need to ensure that the focus moves in a logical order when Tab is pressed. The solution is to set the TabIndex property.

Setting the tab order can be confusing, because when you change the TabIndex of one control, Visual Basic will alter other TabIndex properties automatically. The tab order will remain the same though, apart from the actual control you are editing.

How to set the tab order

1 Place several controls on a form, or open a form you have been working on. Then, from the View menu, choose Tab Order. Small tabs appear on each control, indicating the current tab order.

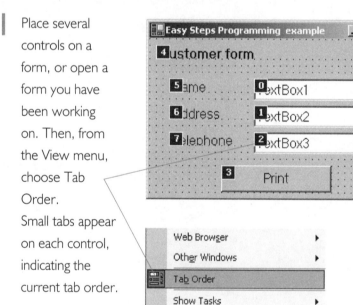

2 Carefully click on each control in turn, in the order you want the Tab order to be. If you make a mistake, you can start again once you have clicked all the controls.

Some other controls

There are several other controls in the standard Toolbox:

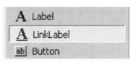

The **LinkLabel** is a label that can contain hyperlinks. Use it to give a Web look to a Windows application

The **MainMenu** and **ContextMenu** controls are covered on pages 92–96. They are used for adding a custom menu to a form

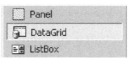

Before adding the scrollbar to a project, check to see if the object for which you want the scrollbar already has a Scrollbars property. Some objects appear with a scrollbar by default. These built-in scrollbars are much easier to work with than the separate scrollbar controls.

A powerful control, the **DataGrid** is covered on pages 125–130. It is mainly for database applications

HScrollBar and **VScrollBar** are used for creating custom scrollbars. The **TrackBar** is similar, but with a different look and feel

The **DomainUpDown** for strings lets the user click through a collection of strings

The **NumericUpDown** lets the user change a number by clicking on small arrows

The **ProgressBar** is for displaying the progress of a long operation

Using Anchor and Dock properties

Users like to be able to resize forms, for example to view more of the text in a textbox without scrolling. It is important to control what happens when a form is resized. Visual Basic makes this easy with the Anchor and Dock properties. Anchor can be set to any combination of Top, Bottom, Left and Right. The Anchor property means "stay at the same distance from these edges when the form is resized". Dock means "fill the area right up to the specified edge". Here are some possibilities:

Typically, you will want fixed-size controls like buttons to be anchored to a corner, whereas controls that benefit from a larger size, such as TextBoxes, ListBoxes or some images, will be anchored so they stretch as the form is resized.

- If you anchor a control to a corner, then it remains the same size and stays the same distance from that corner when the form is resized. The default is Top Left

- If you anchor a control to an edge, then it remains the same size and distance from that edge, but will move along the edge when the edge itself is resized

- If you anchor a control to three edges, it will stretch as the control is resized, so it remains the same distance from all three edges

- If you anchor a control to all four edges, then the control will stretch so that its distance from each edge remains the same as the form is resized. This way you can set a control to fill a form completely

For complex forms, use panels to contain your other controls. The controls can be anchored to the panel, and the panel anchored to the form, enabling full control over resizing. Another possibility is to write code for the SizeChanged event, if the Anchor property does not give enough flexibility.

- If you want a control to fill one side of a form right to the edge, or to fill a form completely, use the Dock property instead of Anchor

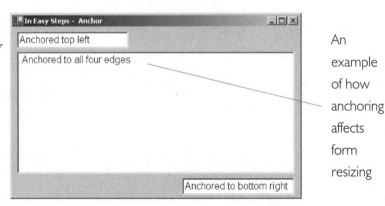

An example of how anchoring affects form resizing

Basic Essentials

Visual Basic lets you do most of your work visually but you still need to write code that controls the visual components. Such code is written in Basic, the easiest computer language to learn and use. Snippets of Basic have already appeared in Chapters One and Two. You'll now learn to write programs of your own.

Covers

Chapter Three

Start at the beginning

Programs are a series of instructions that tell the computer what to do. Although programs can be complex, each individual instruction is generally simple. The computer starts at the beginning and works through line by line until it gets to the end. Here are some of the essential elements in Visual Basic:

The best way to learn how to program is by doing it. Visual Basic is a safe environment in which to try things out and learn from your mistakes.

Statement

This is an instruction that directs Visual Basic in how to run your program. For example, the If statement means do something if a condition is True.

Functions

These are instructions that return a value. For example, Now is a function that returns the current date and time.

Variables

These are words that store a value. For example, the line:

```
myvar = "Visual Basic"
```

stores a string of characters in a variable called myvar.

Operators

This refers to arithmetical operators like "+", "–" and "=". Because it would otherwise be confused with a letter, the symbol used for multiplication is the asterisk: "*". Division is expressed by the forward-sloping slash character: "/".

Objects and Classes

Visual Basic is called an object-oriented programming language, because every element is an object or can be treated as one.

Objects can be visible, like forms or buttons, or invisible, like the Windows clipboard. You can also create custom objects. In Visual Basic, any element can be treated as an object. The code that defines an object is called a Class.

Properties

Properties are the characteristics of an object.

Methods

Methods are actions an object can perform. For example, Forms have a Hide method which makes the form invisible.

An example program

Here is a simple program with an explanation of its parts:

1 Place a label and a button on a form. Then double-click the button to open the code editor for the Click event.

The keyword Dim means "Declare". The best Visual Basic programmers declare all variables with Dim, Public, Private, Protected or Friend. Use the Project Properties dialog, Common Properties, Build section to turn this on or off (it is on by default). This prevents errors such as misspelt variables.

You can find the Project Properties dialog by right-clicking the project name in the Solution Explorer and choosing Properties.

2 Type in the code as shown below, beginning with the line starting "Dim..." and ending with "End If". The rest of the code is generated automatically. You are typing into a "Private Sub" which means a subroutine (Sub) that is only accessible from this form (Private).

This line tells Visual Basic that we are going to use a variable called myvar to hold a string value

What about all that other code Visual Basic generates, like "Public Class Form1"? See the next page for a quick tour.

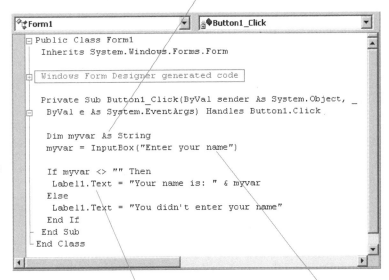

```
Public Class Form1
    Inherits System.Windows.Forms.Form

    Windows Form Designer generated code

    Private Sub Button1_Click(ByVal sender As System.Object, _
    ByVal e As System.EventArgs) Handles Button1.Click

    Dim myvar As String
    myvar = InputBox("Enter your name")

    If myvar <> "" Then
      Label1.Text = "Your name is: " & myvar
    Else
      Label1.Text = "You didn't enter your name"
    End If
  End Sub
End Class
```

Next, Visual Basic compares the string in myvar to an empty string. If it is not empty, the label's Text property is set to the string's value, otherwise a message appears. An empty string is shown as ""

This line is executed right to left. First, Visual Basic calls the InputBox function which asks the user to type in a string. The resulting string is stored in the myvar variable

A quick look at the generated code

Along with the code you typed, Visual Basic generates a lot of other code. You do not need to understand this code to work with Visual Basic, but it helps to know what it is there for. Treat this page as background information, or skip over it and refer to it later if you prefer.

The code Visual Basic generates is needed for your programs to run. If you amend it, it can be hard to fix, so be cautious about changing or deleting anything you didn't actually type.

The whole code block makes up a Public Class. A class is code that defines an object, in this case your form. The next line, beginning Inherits, means that this class has all the characteristics of the class it inherits from: the standard Windows Form class

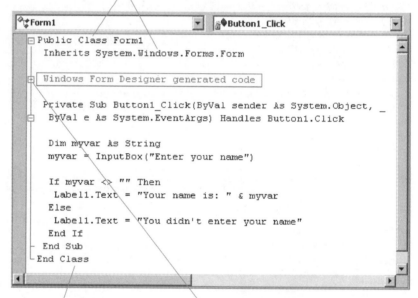

```
Form1                                    Button1_Click

Public Class Form1
    Inherits System.Windows.Forms.Form

    Windows Form Designer generated code

    Private Sub Button1_Click(ByVal sender As System.Object, _
      ByVal e As System.EventArgs) Handles Button1.Click

        Dim myvar As String
        myvar = InputBox("Enter your name")

        If myvar <> "" Then
         Label1.Text = "Your name is: " & myvar
        Else
         Label1.Text = "You didn't enter your name"
        End If
    End Sub
End Class
```

The statement "End Class" tells Visual Basic that the class definition is complete

This "+" symbol means there is code hidden from view, which you can expand. This is the code representation of the buttons, labels and other controls you have added to the form design. When you set a property in the properties window, equivalent code gets written here

Variables/scope

In the example on page 53, a variable called myvar was used to store a string of characters. It is called a variable because its contents can change during the course of a program.

Variables have some important characteristics. One of them is called scope or visibility. This determines which parts of a program are able to inspect or change the value of the variable.

The myvar variable was declared in a subroutine. Variables like this, declared in a subroutine or function, are visible only within that routine.

Variables can also be declared at the class level in a form or code module. These variables usually come at the beginning of a class module, after the Class and Inherits statements and before any Sub or Function statements. If you declare these with Dim or Private, then any other routine in that form or code module can use the variable. If you declare them with Public they are visible anywhere.

How visible should your variables be? The answer is, as little as possible. It may seem handy to have lots of public or global variables, but it makes errors more likely as well.

Other advanced declarations such as Protected and Friend will be explained later in the book.

If you do not have Option Explicit on, Visual Basic will not report an error if you try to set the value of a variable out of its scope. Instead, it will create a new, empty variable. This can cause a lot of confusion, so you should always use Option Explicit, which is the default in any case.

This is a public variable visible throughout the project

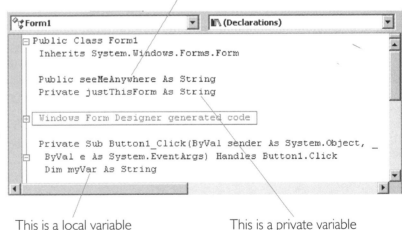

This is a local variable visible only in the Button1_Click subroutine

This is a private variable visible to all routines in this form or module

Introducing data types

Along with scope, another important characteristic of a variable is its type. This determines what kind of information (data) a variable can hold.

Anything within double quotation marks is a string. For example, "123" is a string and not a number. The contents of text boxes are strings as well.

For example, a string variable stores a string of characters. This is useful for things like names and addresses, but is of no use for mathematical calculations. If you want to store numbers and perform calculations, you need a numeric variable like an integer.

If you would rather not worry about data types, you can use a general-purpose type called an *Object*. Objects hold data of any type. To make things easy, variables in Visual Basic are objects by default. To declare other types of variable, you need to use the As keyword. For example,

The word "Cast" means conversion. An invalid cast is an invalid conversion.

```
Dim MyVar As String
```

declares a string variable.

Even object types will not let you do the impossible. For example, you cannot multiply a string by a number. If you try, Visual Basic will report an "Invalid cast" error. Fortunately, there are functions that convert data from one type to another.

Why bother with data types?

Two useful Visual Basic functions are Str(), which converts a number to a string, and Val(), which converts a string to a number. If Val cannot find a number in the string, it simply returns zero.

Even if you begin by using the Object type, you should aim to use specific data types as you progress with Visual Basic. This helps to prevent errors, and lets your computer work more efficiently. For example, if the computer knows the data type of a variable, it can work out the amount of memory it needs to store it. That means it can manage memory more efficiently.

Exploring data types

Visual Basic has eleven data types as well as Objects:

If you are new to computers you might wonder why some of the limits here look like strange choices, for example those for an integer. The reason is that computers store numbers in binary, so limits come in powers of two.

String	This is a sequence of up to around 2 billion characters. You can also declare fixed-length strings.
Integer	This is a whole number from -2,147,483,648 to 2,147,483,647.
Long	This is a whole number from -9,223,372,036,854,775,808 to 9,223,372,036,854,775,807.
Short	This is a whole number from -32,768 to 32,767.
Single	A floating point data type which holds positive or negative numbers up to around 3.4 E38. "E38" means "times 10 to the power of 38" so this is a very large number.
Double	A floating-point data type like Single but holding positive or negative numbers to around 1.8 E308.
Decimal	This data type is for positive or negative numbers with up to 29 digits, the decimal point being anywhere from after the first digit. Unlike floating point numbers, which are rounded internally, the Decimal type is stored exactly.
Date	Holds dates from January 1, 0001 to December 31, 9999. Time information is also stored.
Boolean	This is the simplest data type. It has just two possible values, True and False.
Byte	This data type holds positive numbers from 0 to 255.
Char	This represents a single character or a positive number up to 65535.

With so many different types, you may be wondering which to use when. From the computer's point of view, smaller means faster, so use the smallest data type sufficient for every possible value you want to store. Variables that are too small for your data can cause subtle bugs, so if in doubt err on the side of a larger data type.

Two special kinds of data type are user-defined types and arrays. User-defined types are a group of variables referred to as one. Arrays are covered later, on page 64.

Doing sums

This example program is a calculator. You type in two numbers, and the program adds, subtracts, divides or multiplies the numbers depending which button you click.

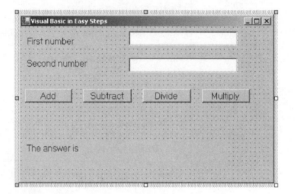

Start a new application with a blank form. Place labels, text boxes and buttons on the form as shown.

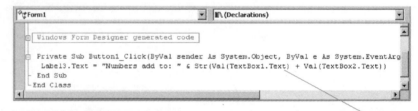

*Symbols like +
and * are used
to make
calculations.
They are called
operators. The four listed
here are the most common.
Sometimes the & operator is
used instead of +, to join
two strings of text.*

2 Double-click the Add button to open the Click procedure. Type in the following line of code on one line:

```
Label3.Text = "Numbers add to: " &
Str(Val(TextBox1.Text) + Val(TextBox2.Text))
```

3 Type a similar line for the other three buttons, but replace the "+" in step 2 with:

-     for Subtract
- /   for Divide
- *   for Multiply

4 Run the program to try it out.

Using If... Then... Else

Visual Basic's If statement lets you add intelligence to your programs, by doing one thing or another depending on a condition you set.

Putting it to work

To open the code editor at the right point, you must double-click the background of the form itself, not the label.

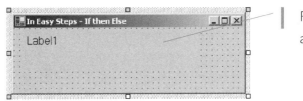

Place a label on a form.

2 Double-click the form to open the code editor at the form load event. This code will run when the application starts.

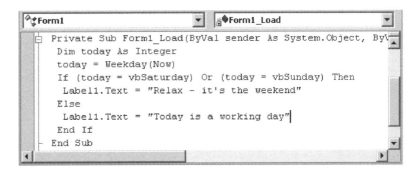

This code uses some handy Visual Basic functions. Now contains the current date and time. WeekDay converts this to a number representing the day of the week. Constants like vbSaturday save you needing to remember which number stands for which day.

3 Enter this code and then run the program:

```
Dim today As Integer
today = Weekday(Now)
If (today = vbSaturday) Or (today = vbSunday)
Then
Label1.Text = "Relax - it's the weekend"
Else
Label1.Text = "Today is a working day"
End If
```

Using For... Next

If... Then blocks let you create branches in your code. By contrast, For... Next creates a block of code which runs more than once.

A For... Next example

This application calculates the annual interest on a sum of money entered by the user.

| Place a label, text box, button and list box on a form as shown.

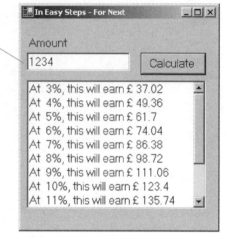

2 Double-click the button and type in this code for the Click event (to use the application, enter a number into the text box and then click the button):

```
Dim curAmount As Decimal
Dim iCountVar As Integer

ListBox1.Items.Clear()
curAmount = Val(TextBox1.Text)

If curAmount <> 0 Then
  For iCountVar = 3 To 15
    ListBox1.Items.Add("At " + Str(iCountVar) _
    + "%, this will earn £" + Str(curAmount * _
    iCountVar / 100))
  Next iCountVar
Else
  MsgBox("Not a valid amount")
End If
```

This code shows how you can nest a For... Next loop inside an If... Then block. Nesting blocks is a powerful technique, but can get confusing if you have too many levels.

Using Do... Loop

Not all loops use For... Next. Two other possibilities are Do While... Loop and Do Until... Loop. Do... While loops until a condition is false, and Do... Until loops until a condition is true.

An example

1 Place a button on a form.

2 Double-click the button and enter the following code for the Click event:

```
Dim answer As Integer
Do Until answer = vbYes
answer = MsgBox("Choose Yes to exit, _
No to continue", vbYesNo)
Loop
```

You can also place the condition at the end of the loop, in the form
Do... Loop Until. Then you can be sure the loop gets executed at least once.

3 Run the application and click the button. A dialog appears. If you click Yes the dialog closes, but if you click No it closes and immediately reappears.

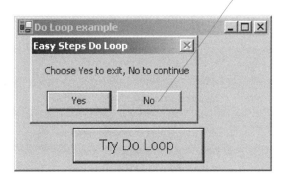

Why are there two kinds of Do loop, when one would be sufficient? After all, you can make a While condition into an Until condition simply by putting Not in front of it. The reason is the clarity of your code. Having two possibilities lets you choose the one that most clearly expresses the reason for the loop. When you or someone else comes back to the code later, to fix a problem or to introduce an improvement, this helps you to understand how it works.

Using Case... Else

If… Then is a good way to create branches in your code, but can be awkward when there are lots of possible branches. Visual Basic has Select Case... End Select blocks, which let you run different code depending on the value of a test variable.

A Select Case example

In this example, note that the line beginning with an apostrophe (')
is a comment which does nothing at runtime. Comments are a useful way to make programs easier to read.

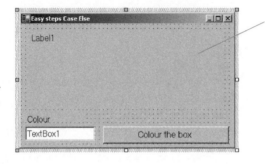

Place two labels, a text box and a button on a form as shown.

2 Double-click the button and enter the following code:

```
Dim sColour As String

sColour = UCase(Trim(TextBox1.Text))
Label1.Text = TextBox1.Text

 Select Case sColour
  Case "RED"
   Label1.BackColor = Color.Red
  Case "BLUE"
   Label1.BackColor = Color.Blue
  'etc ... add other colors
  Case Else
   Label1.BackColor = Color.White
   Label1.Text = "Unknown colour"
 End Select
```

UCase and Trim are useful functions to prevent confusion when
the user types in mixed case or leaves leading or trailing spaces.

A better way to choose colours in Visual Basic is to use the ColorDialog
control. This example is just to show how Select Case works.

3 Run the application, type a colour into the text box, and click the button.

Using With... End With

The With... End With block in Visual Basic is different from other kinds of block, in that it only exists to make your code easier to write and maintain.

It is a way of executing a series of statements on a Visual Basic object. Instead of writing:

```
object.thisproperty = "Something"
object.thatproperty = "Something else"
```

you can write:

```
With object
    .thisproperty = "Easy"
    .thatproperty = "Steps"
End With
```

This is most useful when the object name is long and unwieldy. Most often this is in programs that control other programs through automation.

An example of With... End With

1 Place a label and a button on a form.

2 Double-click the button and write this code for the Click event:

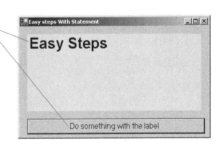

```
With Label1
  .Text = "Easy Steps"
  .BackColor = Color.Blue
  .ForeColor = Color.Yellow
  .Font = New Font("Arial", 24, FontStyle.Bold)
End With
```

Dealing with a set of values

By now you will have got used to the idea of variables, which let you store values while your program is running.

Once you have declared an array, be careful not to try to access elements that do not exist. In this example, if you referred to MonthlySales(20) Visual Basic would report a "Index out of range" error.

Sometimes it is convenient to deal with a set of values. For example, you might want to work on the monthly sales figures for a year. Rather than having 12 variables called JanSales, FebSales etc, it would be better to have a single array with 12 elements. Then you can refer to MonthlySales(0), MonthlySales(1) instead. Here is an example:

```
Dim MonthlySales(11) As Decimal
Dim TotalSales As Decimal
Dim iCountVar As Integer
MonthlySales(0) = 5214.45
MonthlySales(1) = 4576.76
MonthlySales(2) = 7142.32
'etc
```

The biggest advantage of arrays is that you can process them in a loop. For instance, the following routine goes on to work out total sales for the year:

Visual Basic array elements always start at zero. That means the last element of a 12-element array is numbered 11.

```
For iCountVar = 0 To 11
TotalSales = TotalSales + MonthlySales(iCountVar)
Next
Label1.Text = "Total Sales: " + Str(TotalSales)
```

Multiple dimensions

Arrays can have more than one dimension. For example, you could store sales for two shops in one array:

```
Dim MonthlySales(11,1) as Decimal
MonthlySales(0,0) = 5621.34 ' first shop
MonthlySales(0,1) = 5214.45 ' second shop
```

Using Structures

Sometimes you need to store more than one value in a variable. For example, if your application deals with customers, you might want to store a name, address and telephone number for each customer. One approach would be to have three variables, CustName, CustAddress and CustTel. A better way is to have a Customer variable divided into fields, so you can refer to Customer.Name, Customer.Address and Customer.Telephone. You can do this in Visual Basic with a user-defined Structure.

A Type example

This application displays customer details on a form. It uses a Customer variable type. Here is the definition:

This Structure is declared in a form module, with the keyword Private, which means it is only available to other code in the form module. If you want to use the customer type in several forms, you could create a new Basic module and define the Structure in there, using the Public keyword.

```
Private Structure Customer
  Dim name As String
  Dim address As String
  Dim telephone As String
End Structure
```

1 Double-click a form to open the code editor. From the left drop-down list, choose Form1. From the right drop-down list choose Declarations.

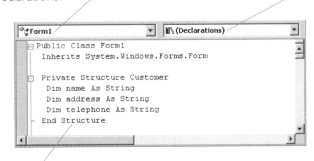

Structures are similar in some ways to Classes. You can even add methods to Structures. Structures are less powerful but easier to work with because you don't need to use the New keyword. An important technical difference is that Structures are value types while Classes are reference types.

2 Then enter the Customer Structure definition as shown above.

Now you can make use of the Customer type in your code. For example:

```
Dim CustVar as Customer
CustVar.Name = "Jones"
CustVar.Address = "4 Park Way, Sometown"
CustVar.Telephone = "01234 56789"
```

Creating a subroutine

When you double-click a button on a form to open its Click event in the code editor, you will have noticed that the code begins and ends like this:

```
Private Sub ... End Sub
```

Sub is short for subroutine. It means that whenever you click the button, this routine executes. You can also create your own subroutines from scratch. Other code in your application can then call the subroutine as required.

A subroutine example

This application continues the example from the previous page. Customer details are displayed in three text boxes. As the application develops, a frequent requirement will be to clear any existing details from the text boxes. Rather than write several lines of code every time that is needed, you can write just one routine that does the job.

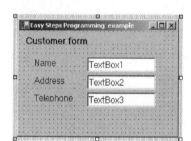

Open this form from the example on the previous page, which includes the Customer Structure, and add labels and text boxes as shown.

2 Open the code editor, and again find the Declarations section. Below the Windows Form Designer generated code, add this code:

```
Private Sub ClearForm()
  TextBox1.Text = ""
  TextBox2.Text = ""
  TextBox3.Text = ""
End Sub
```

3 Open the Form Load event and add the line:

```
Call ClearForm()
```

When you run the application, the text boxes will clear.

Using parameters

A powerful feature of subroutines is that you can pass information to them as they are called. This information is called arguments; the variables they are passed to are called parameters. To illustrate this, and to continue the customer application, the next example is a subroutine that displays customer information on the form.

A subroutine with parameters

Open the code editor and find the ClearForm subroutine from the previous example. After the End Sub of ClearForm, add the following code:

```
Private Sub DisplayCustomer(ByVal Ct As Customer)
   TextBox1.Text = Ct.name
   TextBox2.Text = Ct.address
   TextBox3.Text = Ct.telephone
End Sub
```

You must declare this subroutine as Private Sub, because the Customer type it uses is private to the form module. Otherwise Visual Basic will show an error. If you want to make the Sub Public, make the Customer Structure Public as well.

Amend the code for the Form Load event as below, and then run the application:

```
Dim custvar As Customer
Call ClearForm()
custvar.name = "Jones"
custvar.address = "4 Park Rd, Sometown"
custvar.Telephone = "01234 56789"
Call DisplayCustomer(custvar)
```

See the next page for another example of using a parameter.

Creating a function

When you write functions and subroutines, you are effectively extending the Visual Basic language. This is what makes them such powerful tools.

A function is very similar to a subroutine. The important difference is that a function returns a value. Functions therefore have a type, just like variables, indicating what sort of value they return.

Converting to inches: a function example

This example application converts centimetres to inches. At its heart is a user-defined function declared like this:

This is a parameter to store the length in centimetres

This part indicates that the function returns a floating-point number of single precision

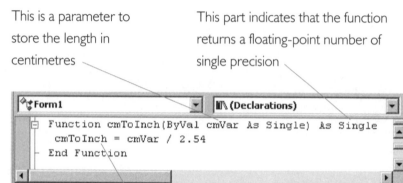

```
Function cmToInch(ByVal cmVar As Single) As Single
    cmToInch = cmVar / 2.54
End Function
```

When you have created some useful functions like cmToInch, you can store them in a code module and use them in any project you like.

The function result is assigned to the name of the function. This is what the code calling the function will get back. If you prefer, you can use Return instead:

```
Return cmVar / 2.54
```

Here is the cmToInch function at work. To create this application, call cmToInch in the button's Click event, passing the value of the text box as a parameter. Use Val() to convert the text into a number, and Str() to convert the result back into text.

ByRef and ByVal

When you look at the parameters in a Visual Basic Sub or Function, you will notice that they are all prefixed ByVal or ByRef. The default is ByVal. If an argument is passed ByVal, the Sub or Function gets the value of the variable. If an argument is passed ByRef, the Sub or Function gets a reference to the variable itself.

It seems a subtle difference, but the key points are:

- If a variable is passed ByVal, and the Sub makes a change to the variable, the change is temporary. If you want the change to persist, pass the variable ByRef

- If you have a large value, such as a very long String, then passing it ByVal is inefficient, because Visual Basic has to make a copy. ByRef is quicker

Testing ByVal and ByRef

If you pass an object ByVal, the Sub or Function gets a variable that refers to the same object, even though it is a copy of the original variable. Therefore, if you set a property of the object in the Sub, it will also change the property in the original object, even though it was passed ByVal.

1 Add 2 labels and a button to a form. Double-click the button to open the code editor. Add the code shown below, including the Sub Doit, and run the project. When you click the button, both labels show "old value"

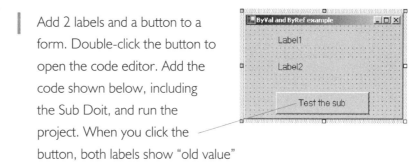

You can get a long way with Visual Basic programming without changing the default of ByVal, which gets inserted automatically.

2 In the Sub Doit, change ByVal to ByRef and try again. This time the value changes.

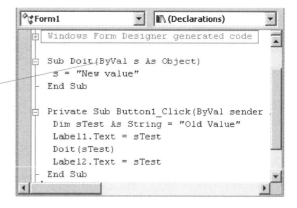

```
Form1              ▼   (Declarations)        ▼
    Windows Form Designer generated code

    Sub Doit(ByVal s As Object)
        s = "New value"
    End Sub

    Private Sub Button1_Click(ByVal sender
        Dim sTest As String = "Old Value"
        Label1.Text = sTest
        Doit(sTest)
        Label2.Text = sTest
    End Sub
```

Using MsgBox and InputBox

MsgBox and InputBox are similar functions which are used to display information to the user and possibly to get a response as well.

Look up MsgBox in Visual Basic's on-line help to see how you can control the title, the number and type of buttons, and other aspects of MsgBox and InputBox.

MsgBox can be used as a statement or as a function. In its simplest form, it just displays a message which the user dismisses with OK:

```
MsgBox ("The operation completed successfully")
```

Sometimes you need more than this from the user. For example, many applications ask for confirmation before printing. You can do this by using MsgBox as a function:

```
If MsgBox("OK to print?", _
  MsgBoxStyle.OKCancel) = MsgBoxResult.OK Then
  'print
End If
```

Using InputBox

When you need more than just a click in response, InputBox provides a solution. For instance, you might want to search for a customer based on a name provided by the user. Here is how to do it:

```
Dim sName As String
sName = InputBox("Enter a name")
MsgBox ("You chose " & sName)
```

Finally, you can provide a default value for InputBox. In the above example, change the call to InputBox to:

See the next page for an explanation of Named Parameters, used in this example code.

```
sName = InputBox(Prompt:="Enter a name", _
DefaultResponse:="Fred")
```

Now the name Fred appears in the dialog. If the user clicks OK, "Fred" is returned. If Cancel is clicked, InputBox returns an empty string.

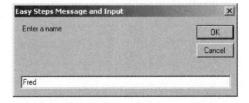

Using optional/named arguments

In the example on the previous page, the InputBox function was called in two different ways. On the first occasion, one argument was used like this:

```
sName = InputBox("Enter a name")
```

On the next occasion, two arguments were used, prefixed by the name of the parameter:

```
sName = InputBox(Prompt:="Enter a
name",DefaultResponse:="Fred")
```

This second technique is called Named arguments. It is used for two reasons:

- To make it easier to read the code and understand what it does

- To make it easier to miss out optional arguments

Another twist on this theme is called overloading. This is where there is more than one function or subroutine with the same name, but distinguished by different parameters. Overloading is common in Visual Basic. An example is the Font class, which has 13 different versions of its constructor method.

If you look up InputBox in online Help, you will see that it has one required parameter (Prompt) and four optional parameters (Title,DefaultResponse,XPos and Ypos). The optional parameters have default values. If no argument is received for a parameter, it takes the default value. In the Function definition, an optional parameter looks like this:

```
Optional ByVal Title As String = ""
```

When you pass unnamed arguments to a function, the function detects which argument is which by looking at their position. The first argument matches the first parameter, and so on. With this arrangement, if you want to use an optional argument you have to supply arguments up to and including the last optional one, so that the position is correct:

```
sName = InputBox("Enter a name","","Fred)
```

In the above example, an empty string is included to fill the space for the Title argument. On the other hand, by using named arguments you can pick and choose exactly which optional arguments to supply.

Printing with Visual Basic

A frequent requirement is to print information from Visual Basic. For example, you might want to print customer details from a form. Unfortunately printing is somewhat complex. There is no single Print method, so you have to write code that outputs text or graphics piece by piece to the printer. However, it is not difficult to get started with printing, as this example shows.

Other print controls include PrintDialog, which lets users select a printer and choose page numbers, a PageSetupDialog control for setting margins and page layout, and a PrintPreviewControl that lets you show previews without using the PrintPreviewDialog.

Since printing is complex, some third-party components for Visual Basic include built-in printing features, so that you can more easily create printed reports.

Open the Customer programming example from page 67. Add a Button, a PrintDocument and a PrintPreviewDialog.

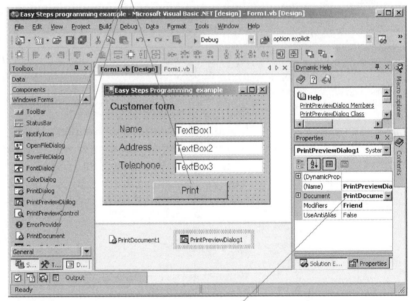

2 Set the PrintPreviewDialog's Document property to PrintDocument1.

3 Add one line of code to the button's Click event:

```
PrintPreviewDialog1.ShowDialog()
```

This code places the lines of text a fixed distance apart, determined by the lineheight variable. For more accurate positioning, you can use the Font.GetHeight method to discover the height of the characters, and add a little extra.

4 In the code editor dropdown the Class list to find PrintDocument1. Dropdown the Method list to find PrintPage. When you click the mouse, the PrintPage event handler is created.

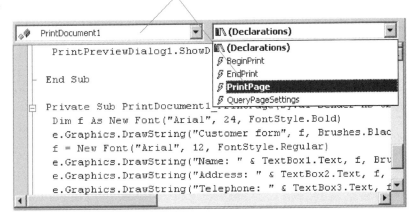

5 Add the following code to the PrintPage event:

This code makes use of the += operator. This is shorthand for expressions like:
ypos = ypos + lineheight.

```vb
Dim f As New Font("Arial", 24, FontStyle.Bold)
Dim xpos As Single, ypos As Single
Dim lineheight As Single = 50
xpos = e.MarginBounds.Left
ypos = e.MarginBounds.Top
e.Graphics.DrawString("Customer form", f, _
Brushes.Black, xpos, ypos)
f = New Font("Arial", 12, FontStyle.Regular)
ypos += lineheight
e.Graphics.DrawString("Name: " & _
TextBox1.Text, _ f, Brushes.Black, xpos, ypos)
ypos += lineheight
e.Graphics.DrawString("Address: " & _
TextBox2.Text, f, Brushes.Black, xpos, ypos)
ypos += lineheight
e.Graphics.DrawString("Telephone: " & _
TextBox3.Text, f, Brushes.Black, xpos, ypos)
```

If you are not sure which fonts will be available, use Arial, Courier or Times New Roman. These come with Windows and are almost always installed.

6 Run the application to test it. When you click Print, a page preview appears. Click its Print icon to send it to the printer.

More about printing

The key to printing in Visual Basic is the PrintDocument. This component lets you set up the page through its DefaultPageSettings property, and specify printer settings through its PrinterSettings property. You can also set the DocumentName, which shows up in the Windows printer queue so that users can check the status of their printout. The PrintDocument also has a Print method, and it is this that kicks off the printing process.

Visual Basic has a broad reach, from beginning programmers to professionals. You don't have to learn every aspect before getting started. Printing is an advanced topic, and not all programs need a print facility, so feel free to skip this topic or to come back to it at a later date.

The PrintDocument knows how to print, but it does not know what to print. This is what the programmer has to supply in code. When the Print method is called, the PrintDocument fires a PrintPage event, passing an argument of the type PrintPageEventArgs that includes information about the page settings as well as a Graphics object. The Graphics object represents the surface of the paper, and has methods like DrawString, DrawLine and DrawImage that let you output text and pictures to the page. The code has to specify exactly where each line of text or image is placed. In order to calculate these positions, there are methods that measure the length of a string of text. Naturally you have to specify the font to use before these will work correctly.

Printing multiple pages

A long document will span multiple pages. To make this work, the programmer sets the HasMorePages property of the PrintPageEventArgs argument, within the PrintPage event handler. It is False by default, meaning that only one page is printed. If it is set to True, then PrintPage gets called again, and so on until all the pages are printed.

PrintPreview

Although printing is complex, Visual Basic makes it very easy to offer PrintPreview. This is good for the programmer too, as you can check how the page is turning out without wasting lots of paper.

Object Essentials

Visual Basic is a fully object-oriented language. Although you can build simple applications without learning about objects and classes, it is much easier if you understand the essentials. Learning object-oriented programming also makes it easier to pick up other languages such as Java and C#.

Covers

Chapter Four

A first object

Objects and classes seem complex at first, but they are easy to use, especially in Visual Basic. To get started, here is how to add your own custom object to Visual Basic:

You don't have to start a new file to create a class, since you can add a class definition to a Form module. Most programmers do use separate files for their classes, since it makes code easier to manage.

1 Start a new project and choose Add New Item from the File menu.

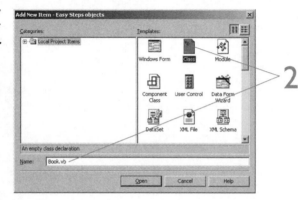

2 In the New Item dialog, select Class and call the new class Book.vb.

3 Visual Basic opens Book.vb and places the cursor after the class statement. Enter the code as shown. When you type Property, VB automatically fills

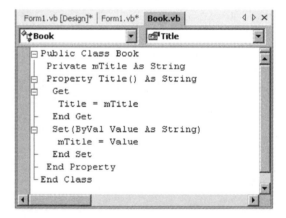

in the outline, leaving you to type the body of the code.

The Book class defines a book, but to use it you need to declare a variable of the type Book, and use the New keyword to create a new Book object.

4 To use your new class, put a button on the form and open its Click event. Add the code below, then run the project.

```
Dim myBook As Book
myBook = New Book()
myBook.Title = "Peter Pan"
MsgBox("The title of the book is: " _
& myBook.Title)
```

Classes and objects

To confuse matters slightly, a class can have Shared members. These are properties or methods that you can call without creating an object. They belong to the class itself.

The previous example is very simple, but it demonstrates several key facts.

To begin with, it is vital to understand the difference between a class and an object. A class is like an enhanced data type; it defines a type of object. It is not itself an object. It is like the difference between the architect's plans for a house (the class), and the house itself (the object). It is a good analogy, because just as you can build several houses from one set of plans, you can create multiple objects from a single class.

The code that makes use of the Book class does two important things. First, it declares a variable of the type Book:

```
Dim myBook as Book
```

Next, it creates an object of the Book type:

```
myBook = New Book()
```

Creating an object is often called creating an instance of the object, or instantiating the object.

This is like the instruction to the builders to go away and build a house. The computer allocates memory to the new Book object, and the myBook variable now points at that piece of memory.

Now you can call the properties and methods of the new Book. This object only has one custom property, although it also has some standard properties through the magic of inheritance (see page 81).

The use of classes to define real-world things like books is called Abstraction, because it summarises the essential characteristics of a book into a few specific properties and methods.

The code for the Title property is somewhat elaborate. The Title itself is stored in a private variable called mTitle. The Property statement includes two procedures, one called Get and the other Set. This means that nobody can access the mTitle variable except through the Property code. You could have avoided this by making the mTitle variable Public. That is poor design though. Using the Property code means you can ensure the Title is valid, for example disallowing a blank title, or making it always begin with an upper case letter.

A smarter Book object

The simple Book class works but does not do much. It's time to enhance it to bring out some of the power of classes and objects.

1   All books have an author, so add an author property similar to Title. That means a private variable mAuthor and a Property statement to get and set the Author value.

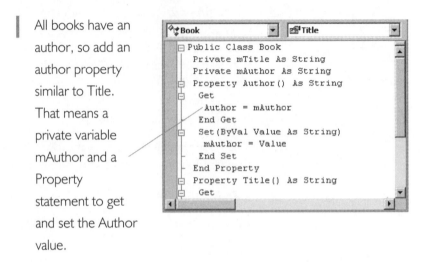

2   Since all books have a title and author, a great idea is to ensure that both these values are set whenever a Book object is created. To do this, add a Public Sub with the special name New. Give it parameters for Author and Title, as below. Note the use of the Me keyword, which means "this instance of the object".

```
Public Sub New(ByVal sAuthor As String, _
ByVal sTitle As String)
 Me.Author = sAuthor
 Me.Title = sTitle
End Sub
```

The New() subroutine is called the Constructor, because it runs whenever the object is constructed.

The code shown will still work if you remove the Me part. Using Me is a good idea though, especially with a common word like Author, since it clarifies which variable it refers to. Another advantage is that the Visual Basic editor auto-lists the object's members when you type Me.

3   When you have done this, you will find the code in Step 4 on page 76 (which uses the Book object) no longer runs. That is because:

```
myBook = New Book()
```

is not now valid. Instead, type:

```
myBook = New Book("J M Barrie", "Peter Pan")
```

You can also delete the third line, setting the Title, since this is all done by New.

New and Finalize

Two critical moments in the lifetime of an object are when it is created and when it is destroyed. The New() method gives the programmer control over what happens at creation. There is an equivalent called Finalize, which gets called when the object is destroyed. However, Visual Basic programmers use Finalize much less than New. The reason is that Visual Basic handles object destruction automatically, through a technique called "garbage collection." Every so often, Visual Basic checks through memory looking for objects that are no longer in use and freeing their memory. The good thing about this is that you do not normally need to worry about the process. What can be inconvenient is that you do not know when it will happen. Since you don't know when Finalize will be called, it is important not to rely on the code there being run. For beginning programmers, the rule is simple: don't use Finalize. There is an alternative, called Dispose(), but even this is aimed at advanced programmers.

If you want to explore a technique not described in this book, like the use of Dispose(), a great place to start is Visual Basic's online Help.

Making good use of New

Unlike Finalize(), Sub New() is used in most classes. The idea is to define New() so that objects are always valid. In the Book example, New is used to ensure that all Books have a title and author.

You might want to allow for the situation where the user does not know the value of some of the parameters in New(). In this case, you can use optional parameters. Here is an example:

```
Public Sub New(ByVal sAuthor As String, _
Optional ByVal sTitle As String = "Untitled")
 Me.Author = sAuthor
 Me.Title = sTitle
End Sub
```

You can use as many optional parameters as you like, but they must all come after any required parameters.

In this case, the sTitle parameter is marked optional. If the programmer creates a Book without supplying a title, then it adopts the default value "Untitled". Optional parameters must always have a default value.

A list of books

A common requirement is to present objects in a ListBox. Page 36 shows how to show a list of strings, but in practice this is often not adequate. Typically, when the user selects an entry in a ListBox, your code needs to retrieve further information related to that entry. A powerful technique is to add objects, rather than strings, to the list. Then when the user makes a selection, you can get at all the properties and methods of the selected object.

All objects in Visual Basic have a method called ToString(). A ListBox uses this method to determine how to display the object. You can exploit this so that Book objects display in the way you want.

It is essential to include the word Overrides when you type this Function.
See the next page for more information about Inheritance.

1 Add the following code to Book.vb:

```
Public Overrides Function ToString() As String
  Return Me.Title & " by " & Me.Author
End Function
```

2 Now add a ListBox to the form in your project, and add a button with the following code:

```
ListBox1.Items.Add(New Book _
("J M Barrie", "Peter Pan"))
ListBox1.Items.Add(New Book _
("Ian Fleming", "Diamonds are Forever"))
'etc
```

Techniques like this are used in database applications, where the list shows a friendly name, but the programmer deals with a code number that identifies the item in a database.

3 Run the application to see the list. The advantage is that if you retrieve an item from the list, say with the SelectedItem property, you can access all the properties of the Book. For example:

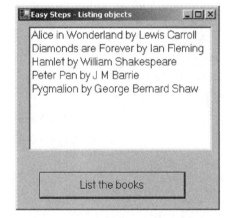

```
Dim MyBook as Book
MyBook = _
ListBox1.SelectedItem
```

Inheritance basics

Another key feature of objects and classes is called Inheritance. This is where one class is based on another class, automatically picking up all its properties and methods. It is an excellent way to create a customised class that borrows most of its features from an existing class. It is important to understand Inheritance, even if you don't expect to make much use of it in your own code, since Visual Basic's built-in classes frequently use it. In addition, all Visual Basic classes inherit from the base Object class.

An example

An audio book is like a printed book, with a title and author, but has additional features like a Narrator. By creating an AudioBook class, inherited from Book, you can reuse your existing code.

In your Book project, choose File > Add new item, selecting a class and calling it AudioBook.vb. Here is the code:

In this code, there are several important features. First, the Inherits statement indicates the base class. Next, Sub New() calls the New() method of the base class in order to create a valid object. The base class is accessed through the MyBase keyword. The code also provides a new version of ToString, so that AudioBook objects are listed in a distinctive way.

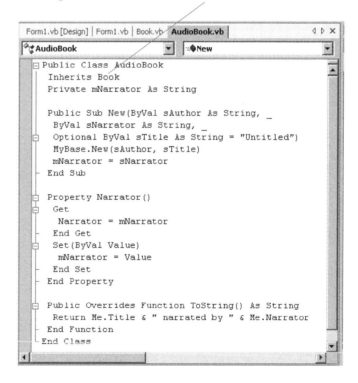

```
Form1.vb [Design]  Form1.vb  Book.vb  AudioBook.vb

AudioBook                                New

Public Class AudioBook
    Inherits Book
    Private mNarrator As String

    Public Sub New(ByVal sAuthor As String, _
    ByVal sNarrator As String, _
    Optional ByVal sTitle As String = "Untitled")
    MyBase.New(sAuthor, sTitle)
    mNarrator = sNarrator
    End Sub

    Property Narrator()
      Get
        Narrator = mNarrator
      End Get
      Set(ByVal Value)
        mNarrator = Value
      End Set
    End Property

    Public Overrides Function ToString() As String
      Return Me.Title & " narrated by " & Me.Narrator
    End Function
End Class
```

2 To test the new class, adapt the Book List project on the previous page to list AudioBooks instead. See overleaf for how this works.

Once you change the type of the Object you are adding to the ListBox, Visual Basic prompts for the correct arguments.

Listing AudioBooks rather than Books does not take many changes. The key step is that instead of:

```
ListBox1.Items.Add(New Book _
("J M Barrie", "Peter Pan"))
```

you write:

```
ListBox1.Items.Add(New AudioBook _
("J M Barrie", "Mary Jane", "Peter Pan"))
```

What it demonstrates is that, although the AudioBook class does not include code for the Title and Author properties, it gets them anyway, because it inherits from the Book class.

Notice how the new list shows the Narrator instead of the author, because of the new ToString() function added to the AudioBook class.

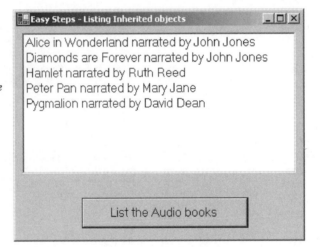

This is the book list amended to list AudioBooks instead of Books

If you want to inherit from an existing class, the important first step is to add:

```
Inherits Book
```

(or whatever the class may be) after the initial class statement. Visual Basic does a good job of prompting for any special requirements in the Inherited class. In this case, for example, you must add a Sub New to the Inherited class, from which you call MyBase.New() with the correct arguments for a Book. Otherwise Visual Basic won't know how to create a new instance of your AudioBook class.

More about inheritance

Inheritance can be chained

You can create a chain of Inherited classes. So you might create an AudioNovel, which inherits from AudioBook and adds special features relevant to Novels. However, you cannot inherit from more than one class at a time.

AudioBooks are still Books

In the rules of object orientation, an AudioBook is a Book, but a Book is not an AudioBook. This means that:

```
Dim myBook As Book
myBook = New AudioBook _
("John", "Jane", "Some Title")
```

This point is important because it ensures that an object always behaves in the correct way for its type. For example, you might have a Car object and an inherited DieselCar object, both with FillWithFuel methods. If a DieselCar object were assigned to a Car variable, you would still want FillWithFuel to invoke the DieselCar version of the method.

is perfectly valid code. An important point: if you add:

```
MsgBox(myBook.ToString())
```

then the MsgBox will display the AudioBook's version of ToString(), with the narrator instead of the author. However:

```
MsgBox(myBook.Narrator)
```

will raise an error, because the Book object does not have a Narrator property. Equally:

```
Dim myBook As AudioBook
myBook = New Book("John", "Some Title")
```

will raise an error, because you cannot assign a Book object to an AudioBook variable. There is not enough information in a Book to make a valid AudioBook.

Casting

As an example, you might have a ListBox that included both Books and AudioBooks. Using code like this, you can detect whether a particular object is a Book or an AudioBook and access the full features of both object types.

If you have a Book variable that refers to an AudioBook object, you can convert it to an AudioBook. Here's an example:

```
Dim myAudioBook As AudioBook
If TypeOf (myBook) Is AudioBook Then
 myAudioBook = myBook
 MsgBox(myAudioBook.Narrator)
End If
```

Understanding Encapsulation

Encapsulation is a feature of object orientation, and fully supported by Visual Basic. It refers to the way that the inner workings of an object are hidden from other objects. For example, the Book class stores the Author name in a private variable called mAuthor. However, no other code can read mAuthor directly, or even know that it exists. At some future date, you could rewrite mAuthor to use a different private variable, and code that uses Book objects could continue to do without being changed. So three benefits of encapsulation are:

The classic definition of object-orientation includes four features: Encapsulation, Inheritance, Polymorphism, and Abstraction.

- It makes code more manageable by letting you break down a project into smaller parts

- It makes code more robust by preventing code from being used in unexpected ways

- It makes code more reusable, by allowing you to change implementation details without breaking compatibility

Understanding interfaces

The word "interface" is another piece of object-oriented jargon. An object's interface is the part that can be seen by other objects: mainly its properties, methods, and events. Visual Basic also has a special type called an Interface. The meaning is similar: an Interface type describes the public view of an object, but without any implementation.

You cannot create an object directly from a Visual Basic Interface. Instead, you have to create a class that implements that Interface, and then create an object from that class. By convention, Interface types begin with I. This is an advanced programming topic, but it is helpful to know what Interfaces are since they crop up in the Visual Basic documentation. For example, the IList interface is implemented by a number of familiar objects, including Array, ListBox.ObjectCollection, and ToolBar.ToolBarButtonCollection.

Overloading and overriding

In the AudioBook class on page 81, the ToString() Function is declared with the Overrides keyword:

```
Public Overrides Function ToString() As String
```

This keyword indicates that the Function has the same name as a Function in a base class, and is to be used instead of the base class version. You can also override Subs and Properties. An overriding routine must take the same arguments as the routine it overrides.

Not all functions can be overridden, only those declared with the Overrideable keyword.

The alternative to overriding is Shadowing, which uses the Shadows keyword:

```
Public Shadows Function ToString() As String
```

Shadowing is risky as it introduces inconsistent behaviour. In this example, if an AudioBook object were assigned to a variable bookVar of type Book, then bookVar.ToString() would call the base class version of ToString(), not the AudioBook version. If you use Overrides, the AudioBook version will always be used, which is often what you want.

Overloading and overriding are features that support what object-oriented jargon calls Polymorphism: the ability for the same thing to have many forms.

MyClass

What if you wanted to ensure that some code within the Book class always called the Book version of ToString(), even if the object instance is an AudioBook? This can be enforced by using:

```
MyClass.ToString()
```

Overloading

Overloading takes place when a class has several functions with the same name, but different parameters. Which version gets used depends on what arguments you supply. The Visual Basic editor shows when you call an overloaded function, by popping up a scrollable number.

You can also overload properties and subs.

```
Private Sub Form1_Load(ByVal sender As System.Object, By
  ListBox1.Font = new Font(
End Su ▲4 of 13 ▼  New (family As System.Drawing.FontFamily, emSize As Single,
                      gdiCharSet As Byte, gdiVerticalFont As Boolean)
Privat family: The System.Drawing.FontFamily object of the new System.Drawing.Font
```

Shared members

Most of the time programmers work with object instances, rather than calling code in a class directly. In fact, normally trying to call code in a class without first creating an object of that class raises an error. There is a way to get round this rule, and that is through Shared members. For example, all books have an ISBN number, part of which represents the publisher. You might want to add a method to the Book class that returns the publisher from an ISBN number. This function is not a characteristic of a particular book, but a general utility. Therefore, you can make this a Shared Member:

In object-oriented jargon, an object member refers to any field, property, function or sub belonging to the object.

```
Shared Function PubFromISBN _
  (ByVal ISBN As String) As String

If Left(ISBN, 6) = "184078" Then
  Return "Computer Step"
ElseIf Left(ISBN, 4) = "0596" Then
  Return "O'Reilly"
  'etc
End If

End Function
```

It is common to have classes in which all the members are shared. These classes are not intended to form the basis of object instances, but simply group together useful functions, types and constants. An example is Visual Basic's Math class, which is part of the .NET Framework.

You can call a Shared Member without creating an object instance, or from an object instance: it makes no difference:

```
MsgBox(Book.PubFromISBN("1840780290"))
```

Code in Shared members cannot access non-shared members of its class. This is because it does not belong to any particular instance of the class. For example, there would be no sense in referring to the Title property within PubFromISBN, since Title is only set in instances of Book.

Shared fields

You can also have Shared fields or properties. This is like a global variable accessed through the class. Change it for one instance of the class, and it is changed for all.

Protected and Friend members

The idea of public and private variables or other class members is straightforward, but sometimes it is better to have something in between. The Book class has a private variable called mTitle, declared like this:

```
Private mTitle as String
```

It is good that other classes cannot directly access mTitle, but it is possible that you might want the AudioBook class to be able to see it. Currently, even though AudioBook inherits from Book, code in the AudioBook class cannot access mTitle:

```
Public Overrides Function ToString() As String
  Return Me.mTitle & " narrated by " & Me.Narrator
End Function
```

This code will not compile. There are two ways to fix it. Either use the public property, Me.Title, or else change the declaration of mTitle in the Book class:

```
Protected mTitle as String
```

The Protected keyword means that mTitle is visible to classes that inherit from Book, as well as in the Book class itself.

Friend members

The word Friend is used differently in other object-oriented languages like C++. You need to remember this if you learn C++ after first learning Visual Basic.

The Friend keyword restricts access in a different way. Anything declared Friend is visible throughout the project, but not from other projects. This is only relevant once you start building libraries for use by other projects.

Protected Friends

It is possible to inherit from classes defined outside your own project; in fact, it happens every time you create a class that inherits from a .NET Framework class, like a Form. Therefore, Friend members may not be visible to inherited classes. If you want a member to be both Protected and Friend, you can use them together.

Visual Basic modules

In earlier versions of Visual Basic (up to version 6.0) a module was a file containing general-purpose Visual Basic code, rather than classes or forms. Modules are less necessary in Visual Basic .NET, which is fully object-oriented. However they are a familiar face for experienced Visual Basic programmers. They are used for the same purpose as before: general-purpose variables, types, functions and procedures. An important difference is that in Visual Basic .NET, you can have several modules in one file, although it is not recommended. In Visual Basic 6.0 and earlier, the module is the file.

Modules are implemented internally as Visual Basic classes with Shared members. You cannot create objects from a module type.

Using a module

1 Start a new project and place a label on the form.

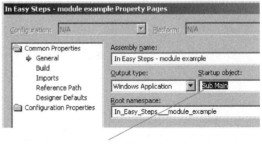

2 Select Add New Item from the File menu, choose Module, and accept the default name Module1.vb

This example shows how to start a project from Sub Main, rather than with form. This is tidier if you want to run code that sets global variables, opens database connections, or does other housekeeping, before displaying any forms.

3 Add the following code to the module:

```
Sub Main()
  Dim f As New Form1()
  f.Label1.Text = "Hello from Sub Main"
  f.ShowDialog()
End Sub
```

4 In the Solution Explorer, right-click the Project name and choose Properties. In the General

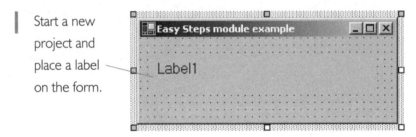

section, set the Startup object to Sub Main. Then run the project.

Understanding Namespaces

In the early days of programming, variables with the same name were a common source of bugs or other problems. It was especially dangerous to use a common word like Author or Title as a variable name. Programmers used to try and avoid the problem by using prefixes or postfixes, such as easysteps_author, easysteps_title.

Modern programming languages are less prone to this kind of problem. Objects help matters, because most variables are qualified by object names, as in MyBook.Author, MyBook.Title. But what if Microsoft introduced a Book class into the .NET Framework, or you installed a third-party library with a Book class?

See the next page for how to simplify Namespace use with the Imports statement.

Namespaces are the solution. A Namespace does nothing except to group together classes so that they have a unique identifier. Visual Basic projects have a root namespace, which by default is the name of the project (with spaces replaced by underlines). If the Book class is in a project called Easy Steps Objects, you can refer to it by the full name of Easy_Steps_Objects.Book. You can also create namespaces with the Namespace statement:

```
Namespace MyNameSpace
Class Book
...
End Class
End Namespace
```

You can use the same Namespace in more than one file, to group a number of classes together. You can also use a dot in the Namespace, as in: MyNameSpace.Bookstuff.

This would let you reference the Book class as MyNameSpace.Book, or even Easy_Steps_Object.MyNameSpace.Book

Edit the root project namespace from Project Properties

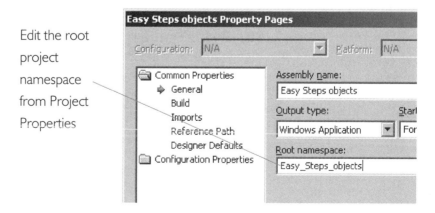

Using Imports

Namespaces are a great way to prevent ambiguous class names, but can make code verbose. For example, it would be tedious to type:

```
myBook Easy_Steps_Objects.MyNameSpace.Bookstuff.Book
```

every time you needed to refer to the Book class.

If you are looking for a globally unique Namespace identifier, a good tip is to use your Internet domain name, if you have one, as part of the Namespace.

The solution is to use the Imports statement. This statement comes at the top of a file, before any Class or Module declaration. It means that any class or other types within the specified namespace will be found automatically, without having to give the fully qualified name. In the above example, you could put:

```
Imports Easy_Steps_Objects.MyNameSpace.Bookstuff
```

at the top of a Visual Basic file. Then you could simply type:

```
myBook Book
```

and Visual Basic will be able to find the class. You can also set an Import for a whole project, in Project Properties.

More about Imports

An Imports statement must use the fully qualified namespace, right back to the root namespace. So in the above example, you could not omit Easy_Steps_Objects. However, you could leave out some of the names to the right:

```
myBook Easy_Steps_Objects.MyNameSpace
```

The word Imports suggests more than just a way of identifying classes. However, that is all it does. It does not load any libraries or execute any code. It follows that its use is always optional. If you don't mind the extra typing, you can always manage without it.

In this case, you could refer to the Book class like this:

```
myBook Bookstuff.Book
```

Finding a namespace

Using Imports does not guarantee that Visual Basic can find the namespace. If the namespace is in your project, there is no problem. Otherwise, you have to add a reference to the libraries that contain the namespace. See page 107 for more details.

Visual Basic Tools

Visual Basic's tools and wizards are powerful but can be confusing at first. This chapter describes essential features like the menu editor, the debugger and the reference manager. It also explains how to set Visual Basic options so you can work the way you want.

Covers

Chapter Five

Creating a menu

Most Windows applications use a menu to give users full control. It is easy to add a menu bar to a Visual Basic project.

1 Start a new project and add a MainMenu control to the form. Next, select the form itself, and check that in the Properties window the Menu property is set to MainMenu1. Click in the menu space at top left, where the words Type Here may appear. Type File.

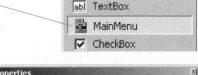

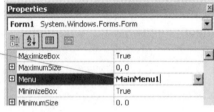

If you put an "&" character before a letter in a menu caption, it will make a shortcut key. When the menu is displayed, the shortcut letter will be underlined.

To make a separator line, type a hyphen character as the Text property.

It is particularly important to name menu items carefully, because with a lot of items called MenuItem1, MenuItem2 and so on it is hard to know which is which.

2 Continue to work on the menu so that it reads File, Edit and Help along the top, and below File, add an entry for Open.

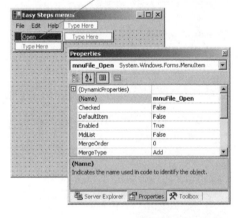

3 Select each menu item in turn, and set its name in the Properties editor. Use a consistent naming system, such as mnuFile, mnuFile_Open, etc.

4 Run the project and notice how the menu you created is fully active, although the options don't yet do anything.

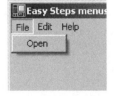

Customising a menu

There are several ways in which Visual Basic menus can be customised. This is done through properties.

The Enabled and Visible options control how the menu item behaves. If Enabled is not checked, the menu will be greyed out and will not trigger any action. If Visible is not checked, the menu will not appear at all

There is a difference between a shortcut key selected from the drop-down list, and creating a shortcut key with the "&" character. The first kind is more powerful, since it immediately carries out the menu action. The second kind only operates when actually navigating a menu. The menu first has to be activated with Alt.

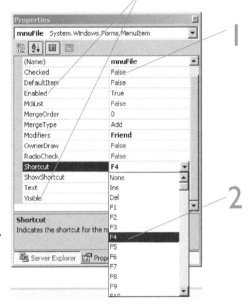

1 Choose the Checked option to create a menu which has a tick mark to show an option is selected.

2 Choose a shortcut key to have the menu action performed whenever the key combination is pressed.

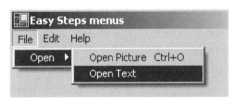

This menu features a submenu and a shortcut key combination

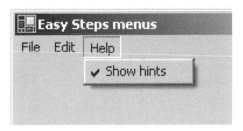

This is a checked menu

Creating a pop-up menu

Windows applications often use a pop-up menu, which usually appears as a result of clicking the right mouse button. The menu which appears usually varies according to what object the mouse is over when the right button is pressed. Follow these steps:

When should you use a pop-up menu? The name Context Menu is a good clue. They are ideal for situations where the user may see an on-screen object and wonder what options they have. It is easier to right-click an object, than to hunt through a range of menu options at the top of the window.

1 Place a ContextMenu control on a form. It appears as an icon below the form, and when it is selected, the Context Menu appears in the menu bar area of the form.
Click on the ContextMenu and type in some menu entries.

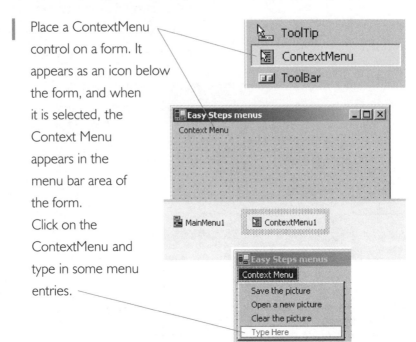

2 Place a picture box on the form. Set its ContextMenu property to the name of the ContextMenu.

3 Run the application and click the right mouse over the picture. The menu you defined opens as a pop-up menu.

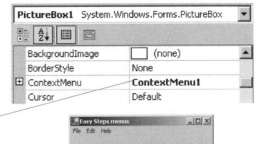

Making a menu work

The menus you have created look nice, but they do not actually do anything yet. This page explains how to write code that runs when the menu option is chosen.

The Sub that runs when an event occurs is called an event "handler". That helps to distinguish between the event, and the code that responds or "handles" the event.

Select the Context menu icon below the form, so that the ContextMenu is visible in the form's menu bar. Make sure you have named the menu items as

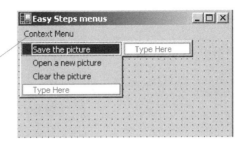

required. Then select a menu option and double-click. The code editor opens at the Click event for that menu option

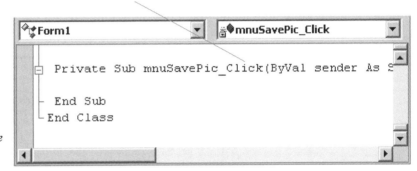

You can use the technique described here to find any Visual Basic code, or to create new procedures and functions. It is sometimes more convenient than double-clicking an object.

If you find this technique awkward, you can also use the code editor directly. Open the code editor, for example by right-clicking the form and choosing View code. Drop down the class list on the left, and select the menu item for which you want a Click event handler. Then drop down the right-hand Method list, and select Click. The editor will move to that event, or else create the handler if it does not exist.

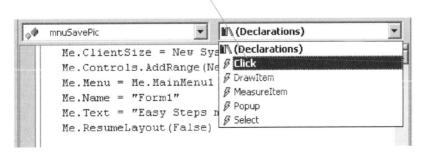

Changing menus at runtime

The best Windows applications protect the user from options that are irrelevant or impossible. For example, a word-processor should not have a Save option when no document is open. The most common technique is to disable or hide menu options according to the current state of the application.

This example uses the application described in "Creating a pop-up menu" on page 94. When you right-click a picture, a pop-up menu appears which includes Save and Clear options. If there is no picture present, the Save and Clear options should be disabled.

The secret is to write code that changes the Enabled property of a menu between True and False. For example, here is how you can amend the code for the Context Menu's Popup event to enable or disable the Save and Clear options:

This code will only run if your menu items have the names shown. You can change the names of menu items in the Properties window.

Open this code by selecting the ContextMenu object on the left, and the Popup event on the right

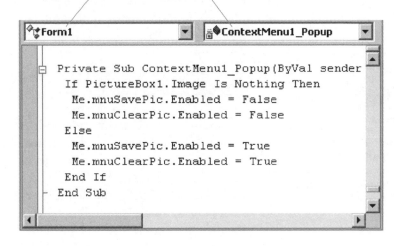

```
Form1                          ContextMenu1_Popup

    Private Sub ContextMenu1_Popup(ByVal sender
      If PictureBox1.Image Is Nothing Then
        Me.mnuSavePic.Enabled = False
        Me.mnuClearPic.Enabled = False
      Else
        Me.mnuSavePic.Enabled = True
        Me.mnuClearPic.Enabled = True
      End If
    End Sub
```

You can also hide menu items completely by setting the visible property to False.

When you run the application and right-click the picture, the pop-up menu will show disabled Save and Clear options if there is no picture loaded. Otherwise, the options will be enabled.

Another useful property is Checked. By changing this from False to True, you can have a tick appear beside a menu. This lets users see at a glance whether a particular option is selected or not, without having to open a dialog box.

Working with the code editor

As you work with Visual Basic, much of your time is spent writing and editing code in the code editor. Although it looks simple, this editor has many features which make your work easier.

If you find these features annoying, they can be turned off using the Options dialog, on the Tools menu.

Syntax checking

When you come to the end of a line of code and press Enter, Visual Basic detects syntax errors such as typing errors or impossible expressions. The problem expression gets a wavy underline. Hover the mouse over the text, and an explanation shows in a ToolTip.

```
Private Sub ContextMenu1_Popup(ByVal sender
    If PictureBox1.Imrage Is Nothing Then
```
'Imrage' is not a member of 'System.Windows.Forms.PictureBox'.

When you work in the editor, the work area can get too small because of other windows. Press Shift+Alt+Enter to hide the other windows and work full-screen. Press it again to bring them back.

AutoList members

As you type a dot, a list of properties and methods pop up. Select the right one and press Tab or Space to complete it. As you select each option, a ToolTip of further information also appears.

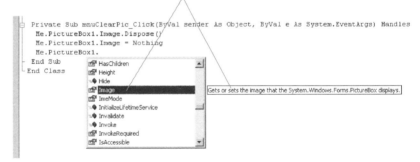

You can summon Quick Info at any time by right-clicking over a word in the code editor and choosing Quick Info from the pop-up menu.

Quick Info

Hover the mouse over any variable or class name in your code, and a ToolTip pops up with information about its declaration and type.

```
    Me.PictureBox1.Image = Nothing
    Me.PictureB
```
Friend Dim WithEvents PictureBox1 As System.Windows.Forms.PictureBox
```
    End Sub
End Class
```

Outlining and auto-insertion

Outlining

The pop-up Outlining menu has several other useful options. It is worth experimenting as this feature is very useful.

The Visual Basic code editor lets you expand and collapse sections of code for easier navigation. By default, every Sub or Function can be expanded or collapsed by clicking on the small + or - symbol. You can also collapse sections of your choice, by selecting them, right-clicking the mouse, and choosing Outlining > Hide Selection. Outline sections can be nested.

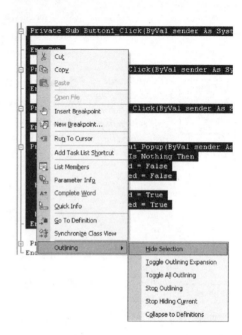

Auto-insertion and pretty reformatting

Check out the Edit > Advanced menu for some great editing tools, including the ability to comment out sections of code, or later uncomment them again.

When you press Return after typing an opening statement such as If or Sub, Visual Basic automatically inserts the closing part. Visual Basic also automatically reformats your code for consistency and clarity. For example, If statements are indented. If you type a Property

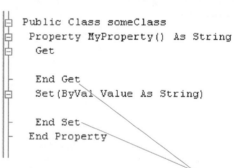

statement, Visual Basic automatically inserts skeleton Get and Set routines.

Dynamic Help

If you find Visual Studio sluggish, then turning off Dynamic Help and other options can speed performance.

If you display the Dynamic Help window (an option on the Help menu), then Visual Basic automatically displays likely Help entries depending on what you are typing or what is selected.

Using the Clipboard Ring

When you are working in the code editor, you will often want to cut, copy and paste code. The standard Clipboard only holds one piece of code at a time, which can be annoying. The Clipboard Ring lets you keep more than one section of code on a clipboard.

1 The Clipboard Ring is a section of the Toolbox. When you start working in the code editor it is empty.

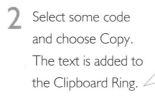

The Clipboard Ring works independently from the Windows clipboard. You could copy and paste from another application without disturbing its contents.

2 Select some code and choose Copy. The text is added to the Clipboard Ring.

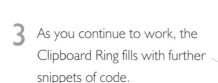

3 As you continue to work, the Clipboard Ring fills with further snippets of code.

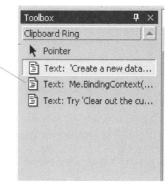

4 To use the snippets, drag from the Clipboard Ring into the code editor.

If you prefer to work entirely from the keyboard, use Ctrl-Shift-V to paste from the Clipboard Ring. By default it pastes the last code copied, but if you press it repeatedly it cycles through all the snippets so you can find the one you want.

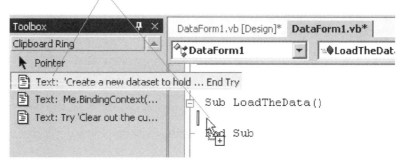

Introducing the debugger

Many programs do not work as you expect the first time you run them. The reason is that computers are unforgiving of typing errors, and just one letter wrong in 1000 lines of code is enough to stop your program working. Other problems are programs that work, but too slowly; or programs that work most of the time, but occasionally produce wrong results.

Normally, the program code is invisible when it is running, but the key feature of the debugger is that it lets you watch your program run line-by-line. You can also pause the program to inspect the current value of variables.

What if your program is in an infinite loop? Press Ctrl+Break to stop it running and open the debugger.

Basic debugging

1 To watch your program run line-by-line, start it running by choosing Step Into from the Debug menu.

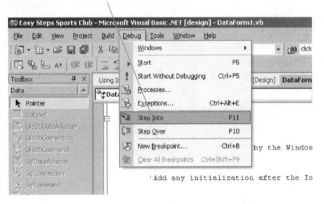

See page 102 for an explanation of other debugging options, including Step Out and Step Over.

2 As soon as the program hits some Visual Basic code, the code window opens with a small arrow showing which line is active. Press F11 to step into the next line of code or Shift-F5 to stop debugging.

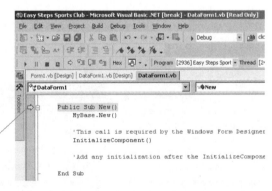

More about debugging

When the debugger is active there are several ways to get information about your program:

1 Rest the mouse pointer over a variable to see its current value:

$$s = Str(iNumOne)$$

2 Highlight a word or expression and press Shift+F9 to open the Quick Watch window.

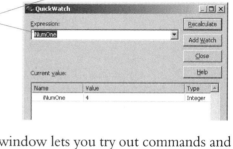

The Command/Immediate window lets you try out commands and test or change the value of variables while your program runs. The Command window has two modes. In Command mode, it offers a command-line interface for Visual Studio. For debugging, Immediate mode is more useful. To enter Immediate mode, choose Immediate from the Debug > Windows menu, or from the Debug toolbar.

Changing the value of a variable during debugging is one way to test "what-if" scenarios, or to fix one problem temporarily in order to continue testing another aspect of your code.

1 Type "?" followed by a variable or expression to see its value. Use "=" to assign a new value to a variable.

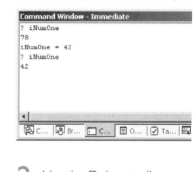

2 Use the Debug toolbar to select the Immediate window, or a range of other options.

Using breakpoints

When a program is of any significant size, stepping through all the code takes too long, especially when most of it is working fine.

Visual Basic lets you set breakpoints, so that the program runs as normal until it hits the line you have marked. At that moment, the program pauses and the debugger opens.

How to set a breakpoint

You can also set and remove breakpoints by pressing F9.

To set a breakpoint, open the code editor. Click with the mouse in the left margin. A dot appears, showing that a breakpoint is set. When you run the code it will pause there. To remove the breakpoint, click on the dot

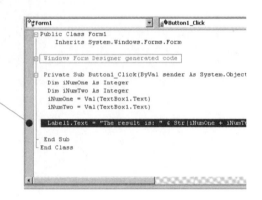

Using Step Over

A feature called Step Out is similar to Step Over. Step Out runs the remaining code in the current procedure without stepping, and resumes stepping at the next opportunity. To use Step Out press Shift+F11 or choose it from the Debug menu.

Imagine you have defined your own Visual Basic functions. If you are stepping through a procedure which uses your user-defined function, then Visual Basic will follow the code from the procedure, into the function (Step Into), and out again. This nesting can become deep as one function calls another. If you want to concentrate on the code in the current procedure, you can use Step Over or press F10 to move through the code. Then, Visual Basic runs the code in the function without stepping through it.

This code is about to call a user-defined function. Press F11 to step through the function, or F10 to run it without stepping through line-by-line

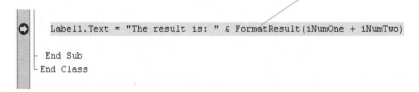

The Locals and Watches windows

When you are debugging, it is essential to keep track of the value of variables. Visual Basic makes this easy with three tool windows:

You can add a variable to the Watches window by drag-and-drop. Select the word in the editor, and drag it to the Watches window. This only works while debugging.

- The Locals window lists all the variables which are local to the current procedure or function in a list, with their values

- The Watches window lets you choose which of your program's variables you want to keep an eye on, and displays them with their values, updated automatically as the program runs

- The Autos window is an automatic version of the Locals window. It shows all the local variables in the current statement and in the three statements on either side of the current statement. The idea is to guess what variables you are most likely to be interested in

Another variation (not shown here) is the Me window, which shows all the variables in the current class, meaning the one which the Me keyword currently refers to.

All these windows can be selected via Debug > Windows.

The Autos window   The Locals window

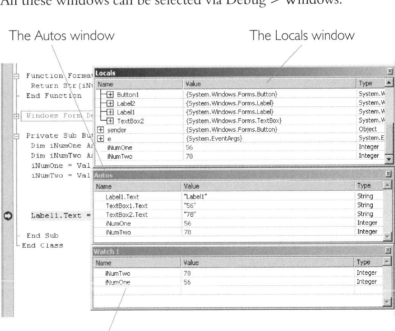

The Watches window

Tracking down errors

Some programs compile and run fine, but fail with an error when certain actions are performed. When that happens, Visual Basic pops up an error dialog. There are several options.

It is often worth noting the exception and looking it up in online Help if necessary

When available, Ignore means ignore the error and try to continue

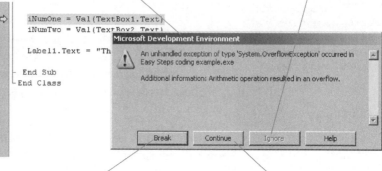

Click Break to go into debug mode on the current line

In principle, Continue means carry on and let any error-handling code catch the error. In Visual Basic, this has the effect of terminating the application

This particular error is caused by assigning a value to an integer which is greater than 2,147,483,647. The problem can be solved by changing the variables to the Long data type, or catching the error and reporting the reason to the user.

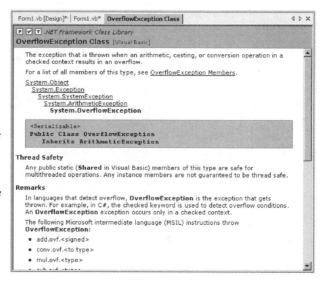

Customizing the Toolbox

One of the best features of Visual Basic is that you can add new components to your project. You can add two kinds of components. Components written in the .NET Framework are one kind, while the other is an ActiveX control.

What is a .NET control?

You will probably find ActiveX controls on your system which you cannot use in Visual Basic. Some ActiveX controls are installed for runtime use only. To use them in Visual Basic you have to buy a licence. Others are not designed to work with Visual Basic. Sometimes a faulty Windows installation prevents controls from working properly.

A .NET control is similar to a Windows form application, but one that is designed to be hosted on another Windows form. You can obtain controls from specialist vendors, or you can write your own with the Professional or higher versions of Visual Studio. If you have the choice, it is generally better to use a .NET control rather than an ActiveX control, since it is likely to be faster and more reliable.

What is an ActiveX control?

An ActiveX control is a Windows executable designed to be hosted within another application. It uses a technology called COM, which is a long-established Windows standard. ActiveX controls are also used on Web pages.

Adding controls to the Toolbox

To use a .NET or ActiveX control, you first have to install it on the Visual Basic Toolbox. Here is how to do it:

1. Right-click the Toolbox and choose Customize Toolbox.

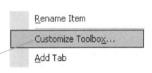

The term component includes visual and non-visual classes. The term control means a visual component you can host on a form and set properties from the properties window.

2. ActiveX controls are listed under COM components. Native .NET controls are listed under .NET Framework components. Check the components required and click OK.

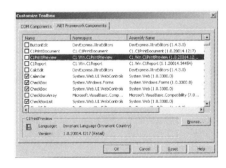

3. The selected controls appear in the Toolbox at the foot of the appropriate section. You can use them in the normal way.

Using the Add-in Manager

Another way of extending Visual Basic's powers is by the use of add-ins. Unlike ActiveX controls, add-ins are not used at runtime. Instead, they enhance the Visual Basic development environment, either adding new features or making existing features easier to use.

Using the Add-in Manager

The list of available Add-ins depends on which version of Visual Basic you have installed. You can also purchase Add-ins as separate products.

1 Choose Add-in Manager from the Add-in menu. A list of add-ins appears. Click on one you want to install.

2 Check to install it for this session. Check 'Startup' to have it always loaded. 'Command Line' is an advanced option for command-line builds.

3 How to use the add-in depends on what has been installed. Some add-ins create menu options, while others extend

You can display the Start Page from the Help menu, Show Start Page.

functionality in other areas. The Web Hosting add-in illustrated above enables simple upload of Web applications from the Visual Studio Start page.

Explaining the Reference Manager

A Visual Basic program is not limited to using objects that are defined by classes in the program itself. It can also use objects in other libraries or applications. In order to do this, you need to set a reference to the target library or application. Once the reference is set, the additional set of objects becomes available in the same way as built-in objects like buttons and TextBoxes.

You don't need to use the Reference Manager to get started with Visual Basic. This information will be useful for advanced programming, or when you want to integrate your application with other products like Word and Excel.

You can set a reference to other .NET objects, such as standard libraries or code in other .NET projects. You can also set a reference to Windows applications or libraries that support COM, Microsoft's older component technology. This is called COM Interop.

A COM example is when a Visual Basic program automatically fills in values in an Excel spreadsheet. From Visual Basic, you can not only put information into spreadsheet cells, but also format the cells, perform calculations, and open, close or print the worksheets.

When the reference is set, Visual Basic loads a description of the objects found in Excel, complete with all their properties and methods. This also enables Visual Basic to check the code that controls Excel objects to see if it is valid. These object descriptions are called "type libraries" and they are loaded by means of the Reference Manager.

As with Add-ins and ActiveX controls, the list of available references depends on what else is installed on your system.

You can also use the Reference Manager to run code compiled with older versions of Visual Basic, 4.0 to 6.0, provided they were designed to support COM.

The Reference Manager is used to add or remove references to type libraries. To use it, highlight the required components and click Select. Then click OK

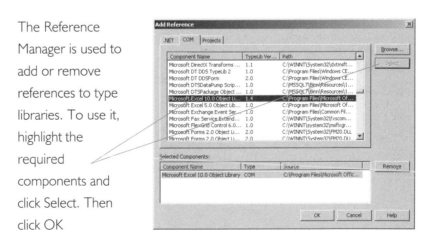

Setting Visual Basic options

The Options dialog is found in the Tools menu. Using Options, you can change the behaviour of Visual Basic to your liking. For example, the Editor tab controls the extra features of the code editor like Auto Syntax check.

Visual Basic's default options are good ones. If you change them, change them one at a time so you can easily go back to the default if you want.

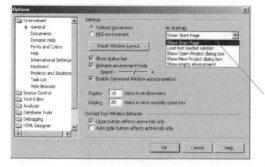

Use the Options dialog to customise Visual Basic to suit the way you work

This option changes what is presented when Visual Studio starts up

Tabbed and MDI mode

One handy option is Save Changes to open documents, in the Environment > Projects and Solutions section. Set it to Save when a program builds and runs, so that you will not lose your work in the event of a power failure or software crash.

One important option is in the Environment > General section. In Tabbed documents mode, windows form a central tabbed section

In MDI (Multiple Document Interface) mode, documents float in the centre area and can be maximized, tiled or cascaded from the Window menu

Setting project properties

The Tools>Options dialog changes the behaviour of Visual Basic, irrespective of which project you are working on. There are other important options which only affect the current project. These are set from the Project Properties dialog. An easy way to find this is from the Solution Explorer.

Using project properties

The project properties are important for the correct operation of your application. Some of the options are the output type (Windows, Console or Library), the compiler options like Option Explicit and Option Strict, the application icon, and for Web applications the target browser type (Internet Explorer 5.0, Netscape Navigator and Internet Explorer 3.0, or Netscape Navigator 4.0). You also set compiler options like optimisation settings and advanced features such as conditional compilation constants.

Solutions also have a Properties dialog. For Visual Basic, the main use is to manage solutions that have multiple projects.

To display Project Properties, right-click the Project name (not the Solution name) in the Solution Explorer. From the pop-up menu, choose Properties. This opens the Project Properties dialog

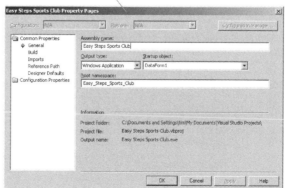

Creating a standalone application

As you learn Visual Basic, you will soon create applications which you want to use without having to run them from within the programming environment. You will also want to make them available to others.

Visual Basic applications are not truly standalone. They use the Common Language Runtime, which is part of the .NET Framework. The Common Language Runtime must always be available.

This page explains how to create a standalone executable. To distribute programs to others, you need to learn about Setup projects, explained on pages 181–185.

1 To create a standalone executable, load your project and choose Release from the Configuration drop-down list. Then choose Build Solution from the Build menu. Make sure it builds without errors.

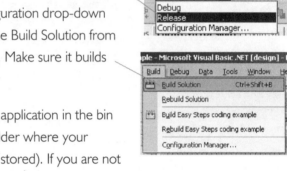

2 Next, find your application in the bin folder (in the folder where your project files are stored). If you are not sure where Visual Basic put them, select the project name in the Solution Explorer and press F4. The Project Folder shows in the Properties window.

The default icon for an application is a dull rectangle, but you can choose another icon from Project Properties, in the Build section. This example is one of the ones supplied with Visual Basic.

If you use the application regularly, but are also still working on the code, it is best to make a copy for your regular work. During coding the latest version may not always be useable.

3 You can run the executable by double-clicking the icon. You can drag it to the Start menu to make it easy to find. You can move it to another location on your machine, provided you move any dependent files with it, if there are any.

Creating Database Programs

Visual Basic is ideal for managing data, since it has a built-in database engine which does all the hard work for you. Data stored by Visual Basic can also be used by other applications like Microsoft Access or Word. This chapter explains how to get started, creating an example database application for a small club. It also shows how to manage database connections, enabling you to add queries and create reports.

Covers

Chapter Six

Introducing databases

A database is simply a collection of information, or data. In a sense, even a list in a word-processor document or spreadsheet is a simple database. Such lists are inflexible and hard to manage once they get beyond a certain size. Visual Basic is able to handle small and large databases easily. You can create forms for searching, updating or reporting on data. You can also use BASIC code to perform calculations or process large numbers of records in one batch.

There are a few words that database programmers use in a special way. It is worth remembering what they mean.

A table

A table is a list of information organised into fields or columns. Usually each field has a fixed length.

The best way to learn how Visual Basic databases work is to create one. That is what you will be doing, step by step, in this chapter.

A table displayed in Microsoft Access

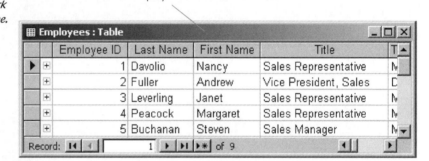

Records or rows

A record is a single row in the list. Tables are sometimes viewed a single record at a time, rather than as a list in a grid.

A database

A database is a collection of tables which are related in some way. For example, you might have a table of customers and another table of orders. Some databases only consist of one table.

Structured Query Language (SQL)

If you spend much time working with Visual Basic databases, you will have come across references to SQL. This is a language used to query and update data. You do not need to learn this to get started, but it is used a lot in advanced database programming, and not only by Visual Basic.

Creating a database with Access

Visual Basic is a great tool for building database applications, but it is a programming tool. This chapter shows how to create a database application, and to do this you will either need to work with an existing database, or create a new one. The next few pages describe how to create a database using Microsoft Access. If you want to learn database programming but do not have Microsoft Access, there are several options:

Access is part of Microsoft Office Professional; it does not come with Visual Basic. Many Visual Basic developers use Access as a database utility. It does not matter which version of Access you use.

- Obtain a sample database in .mdb format, such as Northwind.mdb (or NWind.mdb) which comes with a number of Microsoft applications

- Use a different database manager, such as SQL Server, Visual FoxPro, dBase or Lotus Approach. Any database for which an ODBC driver exists should be useable from Visual Basic. ODBC stands for Open Database Connectivity, and is a long-established standard for database connections in Windows

Even if you do not use Access, you will be able to duplicate the structure of the example database. You will be creating a database to manage a sports club. You can easily adapt it to store general addresses, a book or music collection, or any other kind of data.

If you already have a database you want to work with, turn to page 117.

Run Access and choose to create a new, blank database. In the File Selection dialog that appears, navigate to C:\MYDATA, creating the folder if necessary, and type the name SPORTS.MDB.

2 When the database opens, choose the option to create a table in Design view. The Table Designer opens. Now turn to the next page to continue designing your database.

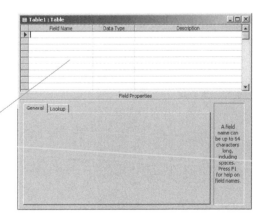

Designing a table

Now it is time to define the structure of the table. This important step determines what kind of information can be stored.

1 To add a field to the table, first type the name of the field in the top row of the grid. Next, check that Data Type is correct according to the table below. Finally, edit the Field Size and Required fields in the grid in the lower part of the Table Designer.

2 Add fields as specified in the table below. Leave any properties not specified at the default values:

These are all standard data types with the possible exception of AutoNumber. Most databases have an equivalent, but it may be called something different. For example, in SQL Server it is an Identity column.

NAME	TYPE	SIZE	REQUIRED
LastName	Text	30	Yes
FirstName	Text	30	No
Address1	Text	50	No
Address2	Text	50	No
Town	Text	50	No
County	Text	50	No
Postcode	Text	15	No
Telephone	Text	30	No
Notes	Memo	n/a	No
ID	AutoNumber	n/a	Yes

...cont'd

The Primary Key is a field or combination of fields that is guaranteed to be unique for each row. Using an AutoNumber field is a good way to be sure that no two rows have the same ID.

3 Next, select the LastName row and set the indexed property to Yes > Duplicates OK. Then select the ID row and click the Key icon, to make this the primary key.

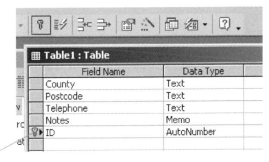

FIELD	PRIMARY KEY	UNIQUE
ID	Yes	Yes
LastName	No	No

The indexes required

4 Finally, click Close to save the table design. When prompted to name the Table, call it Members.

5 When you finish, the Members table appears in the Access database window. Double-click the table to open it. It will look like this, but without any names in the rows.

	LastName	FirstName	Address1	Address2	Town	
	James	Harold	1 The Street	Someplace	Sometown	Som
	Smith	Jane	4 The Way	Anotherplace	Anothertown	Som
▶	Johnson	George	6 The Rd	Someplace	Sometown	Anot
✱						

Record: ◄◄ ◄ 3 ► ►► ►✱ of 3

This page is the last time Access is used directly in this book. The rest of the work is done entirely with Visual Basic.

6 To complete the table, add some names. Add at least 3 or 4, and preferably more than that, so that you can see real data in your Visual Basic application. Click in the blank row at the foot of the table to type in a new name.

More about database tables

Using Microsoft Access introduces some key features of database tables.

Field type

Fields in a database table have a data type, similar to those used by Visual Basic for variables. You need to choose field types appropriate for the data to be stored. Some of the most important are:

Text – for strings of characters like names, addresses and telephone numbers. You can set the maximum number of characters up to 255.

These data types apply to tables in MDB format, the format used by Microsoft Access and by Visual Basic. You can also use other kinds of data tables with Visual Basic, such as dBase format or SQL Server. These have different data types, although similar ones are available.

Integer and Long – for whole numbers. The Integer type is smaller, and can only hold numbers from -32768 to +32,767. The AutoNumber field is a Long Integer. Each record will automatically be assigned the next available number, up to 2,147,483,647.

Memo – for strings of up to 65,535 characters. You cannot specify the length. It automatically increases as needed, up to the limit.

Boolean – for True or False values.

Single and Double – for floating-point numbers. The Double can hold larger numbers and with greater precision.

Currency – for money values.

Date/Time – for date and time values.

Other field properties

Two of the fields, LastName and ID, were set as Required. That means all records in the table must have some entry for that field.

Primary Key

The ID field was indexed as Primary and Unique. It is also marked as AutoNumber. This combination means that every record can be reliably identified by its ID field. This is an essential feature of well-designed data tables.

The Data Form Wizard

The easiest way to display data on a Visual Basic form is to use the Data Form wizard. Note: If the Data Form Wizard is not in your version of Visual Basic, skip this section and turn to page 125. You do not have to use the Wizard.

If you have used Visual Basic 6.0 or earlier for database work, be warned that Visual Basic .Net is totally different in this area.

1 Start a new Visual Basic project. Choose File > Add New Item and select the Data Form Wizard. Use the default name of DataForm1.vb, and click Open.

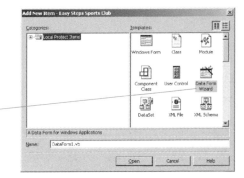

2 Click Next past the opening screen. Then the Wizard asks you to choose a dataset. Select Create a new dataset named and type in dsSportsClub. Then click Next.

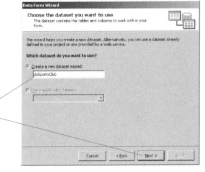

3 The Wizard then asks you to choose a Connection. Click New Connection. The Data Link Properties dialog opens.

Depending on which data providers are installed on your system, this list may look different. The important thing is to choose the most recent JET provider. JET is the code name for the Access database engine.

4 In the Data Link Properties dialog, click the Provider tab. Then click on the line called Microsoft Jet 4.0 OLE DB Provider, and click OK.

Visual Basic's Data Form Wizard will create a data form automatically. It is worth building one from scratch, though, to learn how it all fits together.

5 Click on the small button to the right of Select or enter a database name, and browse to the sports.mdb file that you created with Microsoft Access. Leave the other options at the default values. Click Test Connection and you should see a message, Test Connection Succeeded. Click OK to close the dialog.

6 Back in the Data Form Wizard, click Next to show the Choose tables or views form. On the left-hand side, click on Members to select it. Then click the right arrow, so it moves to the right-hand list. Click Next to continue.

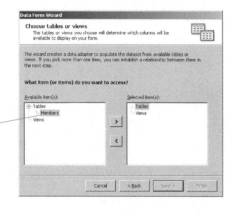

Don't click Finish on this form, as there are some important options in the next part of the Wizard.

7 In the next step, you choose the fields or columns to be displayed on the data form. Leave all the fields checked and click Next.

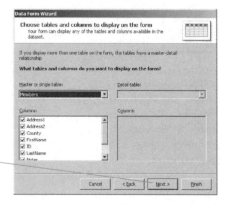

The Grid option uses the DataGrid to show records in a scrolling grid.

8 In the display style form, select the option Single record. Leave all the other options checked. Then click Finish to complete the Data Form Wizard.

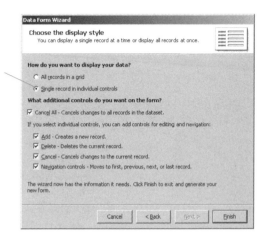

9 If you run the project now, the DataForm will not appear. The reason is that it is not the startup form. Right-click the Project name in the Solution Explorer. Choose Properties. Set the Startup object to DataForm1. Then close with OK, and run the project.

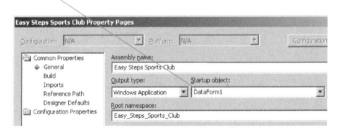

The Data Form Wizard is the quickest way to get started with a database application, but once you become familiar with Visual Basic you will more often build your own data forms for greater flexibility.

10 When the form runs, click Load to show the data. There are forward and back buttons to navigate. Click Add to add a blank record, fill in the new values, then click Update to save them.

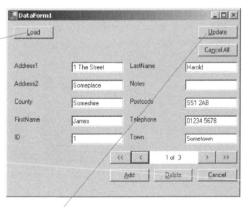

Improving the DataForm

The DataForm generated by the Wizard has three striking weaknesses:

- The fields are in alphabetical order, rather than a logical order

- The records are not sorted

- There is no way to search the database

Here is a quick way to improve the form the Wizard generated. The code is short but not always simple, so there is no need to understand it fully at this stage.

Another idea is to change the Font property of the form, or to make the font of more important fields such as FirstName and LastName bold so they stand out more.

The Search button has its Enabled property set to False, because the search will not work until the data is loaded and sorted. It is enabled in the code for the Load button.

1 Add a Search button and set its Name to btnSearch and Enabled to False.

2 Use the mouse to reorder the labels and textboxes.

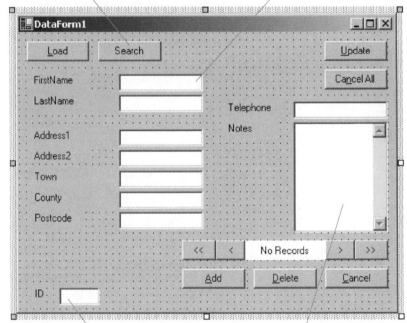

3 Tuck the ID field away as it is normally not necessary to see it.

4 Set the Notes TextBox Multiline property to True and Scrollbars Vertical as it may have a lot of text.

5 Now double-click the Load button to open its Click event handler. After the existing line, "Me.LoadDataSet()", add the following code:

It is important to insert the code at exactly the right point. Otherwise it will not work.

```
Dim cm As CurrencyManager = _
CType(BindingContext _
(objdsMembers, "Members"), CurrencyManager)
Dim dv As DataView = CType(cm.List, DataView)
dv.Sort = "LastName"
btnSearch.Enabled = True
```

6 Next, double-click the Search button (which you added) to open its Click event handler. Add this code:

How does this code work? First, it gets the DataView object which Visual Basic is using to display the records. Next, it uses the Find method to search it. This only works because the DataView is already sorted on the LastName field, through the code in Step 2. If found, the code moves to that position in the datatable. Don't worry if the code seems somewhat obscure – it is!

```
Dim sSearchName As String
Dim iPosition As Integer
sSearchName = InputBox("Enter a lastname")
If sSearchName <> "" Then
 Dim cm As CurrencyManager = _
 CType(BindingContext _
 (objdsMembers, "Members"), CurrencyManager)
 Dim dv As DataView = CType(cm.List, DataView)
 iPosition = dv.Find(sSearchName)
 If iPosition > -1 Then
  Me.BindingContext _
  (objdsMembers, "Members").Position = iPosition
  Me.objdsMembers_PositionChanged()
 End If
End If
```

7 Test the code by running the application, click Load, and then do a search.

What is disconnected data?

Visual Basic's database library is called ADO .Net. It uses a disconnected data model. This means that the database connection is only used when retrieving or updating data. Operations like navigating through the data, or even adding and changing records, can all be done without going back to the source database. Of course, these changes will be lost if your program doesn't specifically update the database at some point.

You can see this working with the application generated by the DataForm Wizard. In this application, the only buttons that cause a database connection to be made are Load and Update. You can use edit records, and use Add and Delete, as much as you like, but nothing changes in the Access database until you click Update. Another option is to choose Cancel All, which reverts the database back to what it was when last Updated.

Only the Load and Update buttons cause a database connection

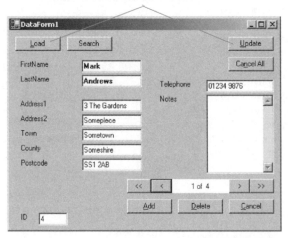

The disconnected database model makes database programming more complex than in earlier versions of Visual Basic. The advantage is that it is better suited to database programs that work on laptops or across the Internet.

The disconnected database model means that Visual Basic has its own database manager. Rather than simply connecting to a database, Visual Basic imports the data into its own database manager, represented by the DataSet object. The DataSet keeps a record of any changes and additions you make. When you want to update the source database, the code exports these changes back. Although it may seem laborious at first, this approach does have some big advantages.

Why disconnected data?

The aim of this chapter is only to introduce database programming. For advanced work you will need other books, or a careful study of Visual Basic's documentation.

The disconnected method of database programming has these important advantages:

- Since Visual Basic has its own database manager, you can program database applications in the same way no matter what source database you are using. The only parts that vary are the connections and the code that imports data and exports changed data

- The disconnected model is ideal for laptop users, or for connecting to databases over a slow dial-up link. Once the data is loaded, the performance is great because it does not use the network

- The disconnected model makes it easy to undo or cancel database edits, because no permanent updates take place until you choose

There are also some disadvantages:

- With a shared database, you will not see changes made by other users until the data is reloaded

- Because there is a time-lag between editing the data, and updating it back to the database, you are more likely to hit problems such as trying to update a record that was deleted by another user

- A badly programmed application may try to retrieve too much data, causing poor performance or even failure

Visual Basic will not save data to disk automatically. You have to write code that calls the WriteXML method of the Dataset.

The important thing is that as the programmer, you are in control. If it is important to do so, you can write code that connects to the source database every time a record is displayed, and which updates the database after every edit. Equally you can have applications that might run for a week without connecting back to the database. Visual Basic can save the current state of the data to disk, so users can shut down without losing changes. ADO .Net is complex, but gives programmers the flexibility to create database programs to suit with every need.

Explaining database objects

If you look at the application generated by the DataForm Wizard, you will notice that it adds three non-visual objects. These are a Connection, a DataAdapter, and a Dataset. The exact type of the objects depends on the type of connection. The example used an OLEDB connection, so the objects include OleDbConnection and OleDbDataAdapter. The Dataset is the same whatever connection is used.

DbConnection

A connection object manages the link to the source database. A frequently used property is the ConnectionString, which has the information needed to find the database. Important methods are Open and Close.

DbDataAdapter

The DataAdapter does the work of importing and exporting data between Visual Basic's Dataset and the source database. It has four Command properties, which represent the SQL commands needed to select, update, delete and insert data.

Dataset

The Dataset is best thought of as Visual Basic's native database manager. Like other database managers, it can manage one or more database tables, which are represented by DataTable objects. When you read data from a Dataset, you do so by reading data from one of its Datatables.

DataTable

The DataTable represents a set of records. It does not necessarily match a table in a source database. Often, a DataTable is the result of a query spanning several tables in the source.

DataView

The DataView is a view of a DataTable. It allows you to sort and filter the records. You can bind Visual Basic controls to a DataView, for a sorted or filtered view of the data.

Showing data in a grid

The DataGrid is one of the most useful controls in Visual Basic. It shows data in a grid view, similar to a spreadsheet. Here is how you can get the Sports Club membership listed in a grid:

If you cannot see the Server Explorer, choose it from the View menu.

1 If you followed the example on page 117, then the sports.mdb connection will be listed in the Server Explorer, under Data Connections. If not, right-click the Data Connections heading, choose Add Connection and set it up using the Data Link Properties dialog (steps 4–5 on pages 117–118.)

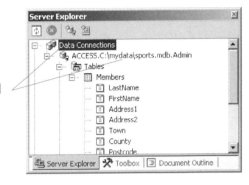

It is important to give meaningful names to the buttons and other controls you use. Otherwise it is hard to maintain the code.

2 Add a DataGrid and three buttons to the form. Set the Name property of the buttons to btnLoad, btnUpdate and btnCancel. Set the Text property to Load, Update and Cancel.

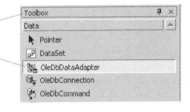

3 From the Data section of the Toolbox choose the OleDbDataAdapter and drag it to the form. The OleDbDataAdapter does the job of retrieving data from the database and passing it to your program. It also handles data in the other direction, sending updates back to the database. When you drag a DataAdapter to a project, it fires off the Configuration Wizard – see over.

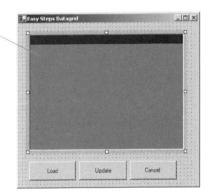

4 From the first screen of the Wizard, click Next.

5 In the next screen, choose the ACCESS sports.mdb database connection from the drop-down list. If you lack the right connection, the New Connection button lets you create it.

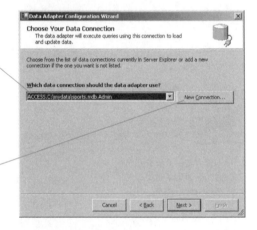

6 This screen determines how the DataAdapter communicates requests and updates data from the database. The two options are SQL statements and stored procedures. Access does not have stored procedures, so just click Next to continue.

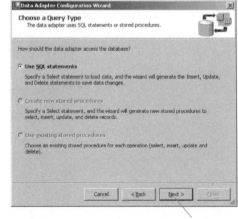

7 This is where you determine what data to retrieve. You can either type in an SQL SELECT statement, or do it the visual way by clicking Query Builder. You can use the Query Builder without knowing SQL. Click Query Builder.

SQL stands for Structured Query Language. It is commonly used not just in Visual Basic but throughout the software world.

8 When you choose Query Builder, the Add Table dialog appears. Select the Members table and click Add. Then click Close.

9 In the Query Builder, check the fields that you want to appear in the grid. They appear in the order that you check; or you can change the order later by dragging the row button.

It's usually best not to include a Memo field like Notes in a grid. Grids are poor for longer sections of text.

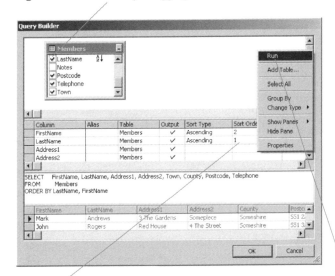

The Query Builder can help you to learn SQL. All the changes you make appear in the SQL language in the centre pane. You can also change the SQL directly, and the results show up in the visual part.

10 Click here to set the order of the data. You can choose more than one field. Here the records are ordered by LastName and then FirstName.

11 Right-click and choose Run to test the query. The results appear at the foot of the window. Click OK to continue.

These steps so far apply for all kinds of database applications, not just those where a grid is being used. What you have set up is a data source that can be linked to any of the Visual Basic controls.

12 When you close the Query Builder, the SQL is copied into the Configuration Wizard. Click Next to continue. The Configuration Wizard shows a summary dialog. Click Finish to close.

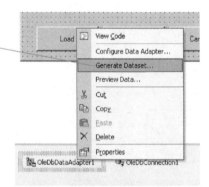

13 Right-click the DataAdapter and choose Generate Dataset. When prompted, choose a New Dataset and call it dsMembers. Leave the option "Add this dataset to the designer" checked.

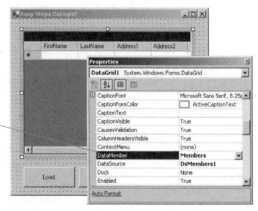

14 Select the Datagrid and set its Datasource property to DsMembers1. Set its DataMember property to Members. In both cases you can pick from a list.

If you try running the Datagrid example, no data is displayed. The reason is that although the Datagrid is linked to the dataset, the dataset itself has not been filled with data. The DataAdapter only brings back the data when the program specifically requests it. Therefore, a small amount of code is needed.

15 Double-click the Load button and enter the two lines of code as shown. Then add the code for Update and Cancel, as shown:

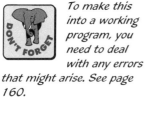

To make this into a working program, you need to deal with any errors that might arise. See page 160.

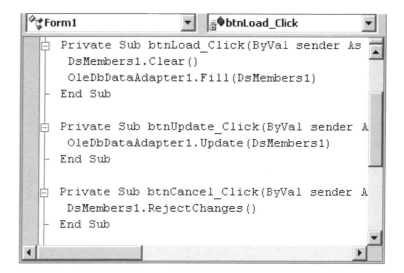

```
Private Sub btnLoad_Click(ByVal sender As
    DsMembers1.Clear()
    OleDbDataAdapter1.Fill(DsMembers1)
End Sub

Private Sub btnUpdate_Click(ByVal sender A
    OleDbDataAdapter1.Update(DsMembers1)
End Sub

Private Sub btnCancel_Click(ByVal sender A
    DsMembers1.RejectChanges()
End Sub
```

16 Run the application and click Load to see the data. Click on the bottom row in the grid (marked with a star) to add a new record. Click anywhere in the grid to edit a record. Click Update to save changes back to the database. Click Cancel to cancel any changes since the last Load.

Cancel will undo all the changes since the last Load, not just the row you are working on. If you add 10 records, and then click Cancel, they will all disappear.

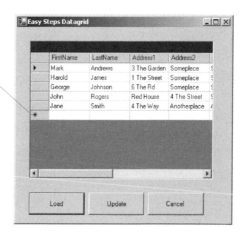

Styling a Datagrid

The default grid appearance is plain, but a feature called Tablestyles makes it easy to produce clearer, more attractive formats. Here is how to use Tablestyles to enhance the example Datagrid application:

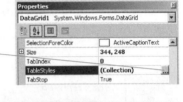

1 Select a Datagrid, and in the Properties window click the small button to open the editor for the Tablestyles collection.

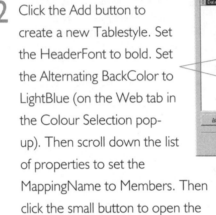

The key to success when working with TableStyle and ColumnStyle objects is to use the right MappingName. If you are not getting the right results, check the MappingNames.

2 Click the Add button to create a new Tablestyle. Set the HeaderFont to bold. Set the Alternating BackColor to LightBlue (on the Web tab in the Colour Selection pop-up). Then scroll down the list of properties to set the MappingName to Members. Then click the small button to open the GridColumnCollection editor.

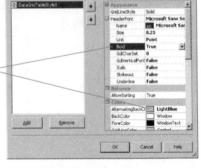

If you apply a Tablestyle, the only columns that appear are those for which a GridColumnStyle is included. If you don't add the GridColumnStyles, you can end up with a grid that does not display any columns at all.

3 In the GridColumnCollection editor, click Add for each field you want to appear in the grid. Set the MappingName to the field required. OK the editors and run to see the new Grid.

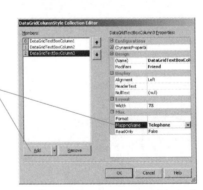

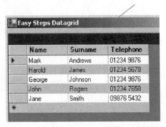

Dealing with large databases

The example Datagrid application works well for a small database, but if you have thousands or even hundreds of thousands of rows it will either become very slow or fail completely. The secret of fast database applications is to limit the amount of data travelling between your program and the database.

The SQL Where clause

To save typing errors, you can use the Query Builder to generate SQL and copy it to your code. SQL statements are not case-sensitive, although the values in the WHERE clause may be case-sensitive with some databases.

You can reduce the amount of data returned by the DataAdapter by adding a Where clause to its SQL Select statement. For example, you could add the following line to the code for loading the data:

```
OleDbDataAdapter1.SelectCommand.CommandText = _
"SELECT FirstName, LastName, Address1, Address2,
Town, County, Postcode, Telephone, ID " & _
 "FROM Members WHERE LastName like 'A%' " & _
ORDER BY LastName, FirstName"
```

If you add this before calling the Fill method, then only those members with names beginning A will be returned. To make this more useful, you could set up a function with the criteria letter passed in as an argument. You could have the user type in the search letter, or have a row of buttons with a letter of the alphabet on each button, so the user could return all the names matching the button pressed. With a very large database, you could restrict the results still further by using a longer string, or insisting that the user enters a complete LastName before any results are returned.

Limiting Fields

Another way to reduce the amount of data is by selecting fewer fields. For example, you could have a separate button to show the full address of a member, and limit the grid to just FirstName, LastName, Telephone and ID. However much you limit the fields, it is important to include the Primary Key, in this case the ID field. Otherwise you will not be able to look up other data about the selected row, or update the data, because there is no unique identifier.

Copying a record to the Clipboard

A handy technique if you have a database of addresses is to be able to copy an address to the Windows Clipboard. Then you can easily paste it into a document, for example a letter.

The Clipboard object

Visual Basic has an invisible Clipboard object. It has methods for setting or retrieving its contents. In this example, all you need is the SetDataObject method, which adds data to the clipboard.

The example also shows how to get the data in the selected row programmatically. Once you know the index of the selected row, you can drill down to that row in the DataSet. The DataSet has a Tables collection, which in this case has only one Table, so it must be index 0. Each Table has a Rows collection, and each row has a collection of fields.

Adding a Clipboard button

1. Add a button named "cbClip" to the data form and give it the Text "Clip".

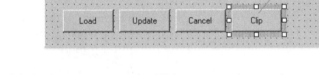

This example shows how to place text on the clipboard that will disappear when the application exits. If you add a second argument to SetDataObject, and make it True, then the data persists on the clipboard until specifically cleared.

2. Double-click the button to open its Click event, and enter the following code:

```
Dim sAddress As String
Dim i As Integer = DataGrid1.CurrentRowIndex
If i <> -1 Then
  With DsMembers1.Tables(0).Rows(i)
    sAddress = .Item("FirstName") + " "
    sAddress += .Item("LastName") + vbCrLf
    sAddress += .Item("Address1") + vbCrLf
    'add other fields as needed
  End With
  Clipboard.SetDataObject(sAddress)
  MsgBox("The address is on the clipboard")
End If
```

Creating a report

One essential element of most database projects is a report facility. For example, a sports club might want to print out a member list. Visual Studio comes with an integrated report designer. Here is an example of how to create a telephone list:

Visual Basic Standard edition does not include Crystal Reports. You need at least Visual Studio Professional.

1 To add a report to a project, choose File > Add new item, and select Crystal Report.

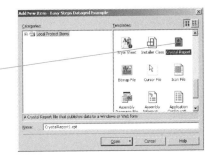

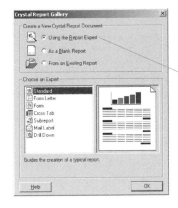

2 When the Crystal Report gallery appears, choose Standard and Using the Report Expert. Then click OK.

3 In the Data tab of the Report Expert, click the + sign by OLE DB to open the OLE DB Provider dialog. Select the JET 4.0 provider and click Next.

There are plenty of other options for datasources. You can link a report to a dataset, but to do so involves a little more code than selecting an independent source.

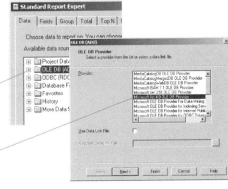

4 Click the small Browse button and select sports.mdb. Then click Finish.

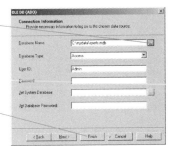

LIVERPOOL JOHN MOORES UNIVERSITY
LEARNING SERVICES

5 Select the Members table from your new OLE DB connection and click Insert Table. Then click Next to continue.

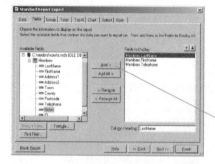

6 Select the fields to display by highlighting the required field in the left-hand list, and clicking Add. For the telephone list, select LastName, FirstName and Telephone. Then click Finish.

Once the database connection has been made, designing a report is like designing a form. Use the Properties editor to edit report objects. Display the Field Explorer to drag-and-drop new report objects, such as additional fields. Right-click the report for a menu of further tools, including sort order. When you are done, save the report.

If the Field Explorer is not visible, show it by selecting View > Other Windows > Document Outline.

Field Explorer   Designer

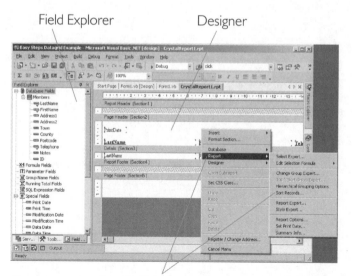

Pop-up menu, choose Report > Sort Records to sort

Showing a report

For really good-looking reports, you can also add lines and graphics. More advanced options include groups, subgroups, and formulae for calculated fields.

1 To show a report in a Visual Basic application, first add a new form for the report, using File > Add new item and choosing Windows Form. On the form, place a CrystalReportViewer object. Set its Dock property to Fill.

2 Select the CrystalReportViewer, and in the Properties window select ReportSource. Choose Browse, and select the report you designed.

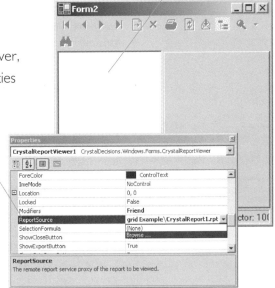

3 On another form in your application, place a Report button. Double-click to open its Click event handler, and add the following code:

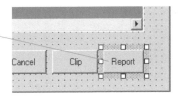

```
Dim f As New Form2()
f.Show()
```

4 Run the project, and click the button to show the report.

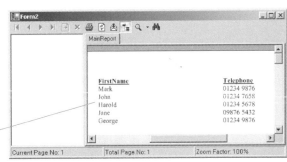

The next step with databases

Visual Basic is a little harder to use than standalone database applications like Microsoft Access, but has several advantages. One is that many of Visual Basic's general development features are also useful in database projects. Another advantage is that if you want to distribute a completed database application, it is easier to do so with Visual Basic. The lack of interactive features in Visual Basic can actually be an advantage, if you want a database application which limits the user's actions to ones that you know are safe for the data.

Working with Access

Visual Basic and Microsoft Access make excellent partners. You can use Access to create databases, set up validation rules, and do interactive editing, while using Visual Basic to develop a packaged application.

The MSDE Database engine comes with all versions of Visual Basic. It is a cut-down edition of SQL Server.

Getting relational

More advanced databases use several linked tables. For example, a company might use separate tables for customers, orders and products. A database for a CD collection might have tables for CDs, Tracks and Artists. These relational databases give more power and flexibility, but are substantially harder to manage than single-table databases like the Sports Club example.

Going Client-Server

Visual Basic supports several database technologies, including ADO.NET, OLE DB, and ODBC. ODBC stands for Open DataBase Connectivity. To connect to a particular database, you need a suitable ODBC driver. Most major database managers have suitable drivers, from heavyweights like Oracle to open-source alternatives like MySQL.

You can connect to server database systems like SQL Server, Oracle or DB2. This is the most complex type of database programming, but is necessary for good performance on large networks, say of 10 or more users.

Visual Basic can keep pace with all your database needs, from small one-user applications to heavyweight client-server systems.

Visual Basic and the Internet

Everyone seems to be on the Web today, and this chapter shows how Visual Basic makes it possible to build exciting Web projects. Using Visual Basic script, you can create dynamic Web pages. You can also create rich database applications using Web Forms, also known as ASP .Net.

Covers

Chapter Seven

What kind of Web?

A Web is any system where Web browsers can view HTML pages over a network. HTML stands for HyperText Markup Language, and it lets you easily move from one page to another by clicking 'hot-links'. The best known network of this kind is the Internet, home of the World Wide Web. But there are different ways in which Web technology is used:

- You may have a private network which includes a Web server. This is called an Intranet

- You may be creating Web pages for the World Wide Web, which you upload to an ISP (Internet Service Provider) to make them available for public view

- You may be part of an organisation with a permanent link to the Internet

Web pages are not always static documents but can also allow you to query databases, place orders or play games. Most things that can be done with traditional applications can also be done on Web pages. There are 3 ways to program Web pages with Visual Basic:

- Write scripts for Internet Explorer. This works from any Web server, but not with Netscape or other browsers

- Write Active Server Pages (ASP). This normally requires a Windows Web server, but can work with any browser. These use VB Script

- Write Web Forms, also known as ASP .Net pages. These are faster and more powerful than ASP pages. A Windows Web server with the .Net Framework installed is needed

A problem with the Internet is that different browser versions and computer platforms make it hard to create Web pages that have the same features everywhere. If you are using an Intranet, it is easier to control what browsers your users have. Some of Visual Basic's Web features only work with Internet Explorer, and not Netscape Navigator. This is OK on an Intranet but not on the World Wide Web. If you are using Web Forms, you can set the Target Schema for maximum compatibility.

A Visual Basic Web form page

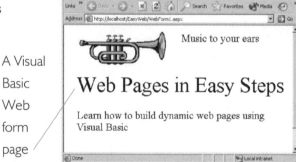

The basics of Web scripting

JavaScript is also known as JScript or EcmaScript. The reason is that the JavaScript name belongs to Netscape. JavaScript is quite different from Java, another programming language, despite its similar name.

HTML was designed as a document format that you could view on different computer platforms and which included the ability to click on 'hot-links' to move from one page to another. HTML has also developed extra features that make it possible to use it for applications, as you would use a Visual Basic form.

HTML pages are stored as simple text together with tags (keywords in angle brackets) that have special meaning to the Web browser, or in some cases to the Web server on which the pages are stored.

Even early versions of HTML support simple forms with checkboxes, text fields and buttons. Before Web scripts were introduced, almost the only thing such forms could do was to send the contents of the completed form to a Web server for processing. When scripting was added, it was possible to run scripts as well, short programs which run on the Web browser's system to automate a process or to provide dynamic content or animation.

VB Script and JavaScript

There are two widely used scripting languages for Web pages. VB (Visual Basic) Script was designed by Microsoft and is similar to the full Visual Basic, but with cut-down features. Visual Basic Script is supported by Microsoft Internet Explorer 3.0 and later versions. JavaScript was designed by Netscape and is supported by both Internet Explorer and Netscape Navigator.

A simple rule of thumb is that you should use JavaScript if you want scripts to run on browsers over the World Wide Web. If you are developing an Intranet where everyone uses Internet Explorer, then using VB Script is no problem.

Despite the above, it is possible to use Visual Basic and have Web pages viewed by Netscape Navigator. You do this by running the programs on the Web server and not on the browser. See page 150 for more information.

Browser programming and Web Forms

Programming VB Script in the browser, and programming Web Forms, are very different approaches. This chapter introduces both topics. If you are mainly interested in Web Forms, turn to page 150.

A first Web page script

> Run Notepad. Type in the script as shown:

HTML header information, necessary for Web browsers to recognise the file as proper HTML

This indicates the start of a HTML form

```
vbs.html - Notepad
File  Edit  Search  Help
<HTML><HEAD><TITLE>VB Script
example</TITLE></HEAD>
<BODY>
<H1>Welcome to VB Script</H1>
 Click the button to see a message appear.<P>

<FORM NAME ="myform">
<INPUT TYPE="text" NAME="txMsg" SIZE="50">
<P>
<INPUT TYPE="button" NAME="cbMsg" VALUE="Click
here">
</FORM>

<SCRIPT LANGUAGE ="VBS">
Sub cbMsg_OnClick
myform.txMsg.Value = "Hello from VB Script"
End Sub
</SCRIPT>
</BODY></HTML>
```

This is the VB Script subroutine. The name of the procedure determines when it runs

These lines define a HTML text field and button

> Save the script as C:\VBS.HTML. Run Internet Explorer, type C:\VBS.HTML in the address box and press Enter. Click the button to try the script.

More about VB Script

In HTML, closing tags are the same as opening tags, but with a "/" prefix.

Where to place VB Script

You can include VB Script anywhere on a Web page as long as it is enclosed in an opening and closing <SCRIPT> tag, with the language set to "VBS" as in the example on the previous page.

How to write script that responds to events

You create scripts that respond to events by naming the procedure according to the event. The rule is that if the procedure is called:

```
Sub MyObject_MyEvent
```

There are other ways to connect events to scripts, but this is the easiest to start with.

then it will run whenever MyEvent occurs for MyObject. HTML buttons have an onClick event, so a routine to respond to a button click is called:

```
Sub MyButton_onClick
```

What events are available?

The following table lists common events which work with most HTML controls. Many other events are available for particular objects and browsers.

VB Script is a subset of the full Visual Basic. For security reasons, it lacks functions to read and write files. All variables are of the variant type, and you cannot call the Windows API. There are many other differences, but the fundamentals of the language are the same.

onBlur	Object loses focus
onChange	Text changes
onClick	Object is clicked
onFocus	Object gets focus
onSelect	Text is selected
onMouseOver	Mouse passes over object
onSubmit	Form is submitted

How do you create global variables?

Declare a variable with Dim outside a procedure to make it visible throughout the <SCRIPT> block. Declare it with Public to make it visible to all scripts in the document.

A VB Script quiz example

This example uses several VB Script techniques, including a script-level variable, radio buttons, and an 'if – then' condition. As with the last example, the script is created in Notepad, saved as a file with a .HTM or .HTML extension, and run by opening it in Internet Explorer.

1 The first part of the script begins with a HTML header as in the previous example.

2 This part of the form will be rendered as text, with the <H1> tag indicating a heading.

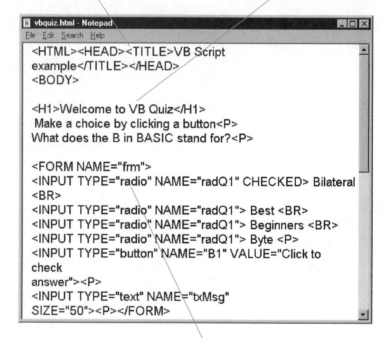

```
vbquiz.html - Notepad
File  Edit  Search  Help

<HTML><HEAD><TITLE>VB Script
example</TITLE></HEAD>
<BODY>

<H1>Welcome to VB Quiz</H1>
 Make a choice by clicking a button<P>
What does the B in BASIC stand for?<P>

<FORM NAME="frm">
<INPUT TYPE="radio" NAME="radQ1" CHECKED> Bilateral
<BR>
<INPUT TYPE="radio" NAME="radQ1"> Best <BR>
<INPUT TYPE="radio" NAME="radQ1"> Beginners <BR>
<INPUT TYPE="radio" NAME="radQ1"> Byte <P>
<INPUT TYPE="button" NAME="B1" VALUE="Click to
check
answer"><P>
<INPUT TYPE="text" NAME="txMsg"
SIZE="50"><P></FORM>
```

3 Next, a form is defined. INPUT TYPE="radio" defines a radio button. The NAME attribute is important – all radio buttons with the same name are in the same group. When you check one, any other checked button will automatically become unchecked. The CHECKED attribute means it is checked when first displayed.

4 Two additional INPUT controls define a button and a text area respectively. The button will be used to find out whether the answer is correct, and the text area to display a message.

5 The next part of the document is the Visual Basic script. It begins by defining a variable outside any procedure. This makes it a script-level variable that remains visible and valid after the procedure runs.

HTML radio buttons are counted from 0, so Item(2) is the third radio button in the group.

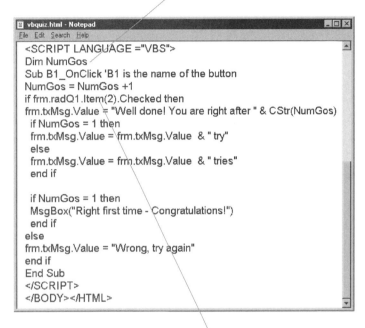

```
vbquiz.html - Notepad
File  Edit  Search  Help
<SCRIPT LANGUAGE ="VBS">
Dim NumGos
Sub B1_OnClick 'B1 is the name of the button
NumGos = NumGos +1
if frm.radQ1.Item(2).Checked then
frm.txMsg.Value = "Well done! You are right after " & CStr(NumGos)
  if NumGos = 1 then
  frm.txMsg.Value = frm.txMsg.Value  & " try"
  else
  frm.txMsg.Value = frm.txMsg.Value  & " tries"
  end if

  if NumGos = 1 then
  MsgBox("Right first time - Congratulations!")
  end if
else
frm.txMsg.Value = "Wrong, try again"
end if
End Sub
</SCRIPT>
</BODY></HTML>
```

You can use MsgBox even within a HTML script.

6 This key line tests the Checked property of the third radio button.

VB Script only works in Internet Explorer, so do not try this with Netscape Navigator. For that, use JavaScript instead.

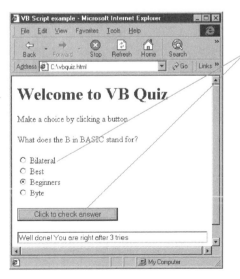

```
VB Script example - Microsoft Internet Explorer
File  Edit  View  Favorites  Tools  Help
Back  Forward  Stop  Refresh  Home  Search
Address  C:\vbquiz.html              Go   Links

Welcome to VB Quiz

Make a choice by clicking a button

What does the B in BASIC stand for?

  ○ Bilateral
  ○ Best
  ● Beginners
  ○ Byte

  [Click to check answer]

Well done! You are right after 3 tries

                        My Computer
```

7 View the page in Internet Explorer to try the quiz. Check a choice and then click the button.

Scripting the Explorer object

One of the most useful features of VB Script is that you can program Internet Explorer itself. You do not need to take any special steps. In your code, simply refer to built-in objects like Window, Document and Navigator. Try the following techniques:

This script detects the browser version and displays a message when the page loads:

You can also inspect the code name and user agent of the browser, in the appCodeName and UserAgent properties.

```
Sub Window_OnLoad
frm.txBrowser.Value = Navigator.AppName & " " &
Navigator.AppVersion
msgbox "Welcome to my web page"
End Sub
```

To program a colour, you can either specify a colour name, or a code giving a hexadecimal value like #FFFF00.

This script changes the background colour of the page:

```
Sub cbChangeColour_Onclick
Document.BgColor = "fuschia"
End Sub
```

...cont'd

To make these scripts work, you need to add buttons with matching names, as in the complete examples located on pages 142–143.

3 This script displays a prompt and then navigates to the chosen destination:

```
Sub cbGoSomewhere_OnClick
NewInput = Window.Prompt("Navigate to
where?","C:\VBQUIZ.HTML")
   if NewInput <> "" then
 Window.Navigate(NewInput)
 end if
end sub
```

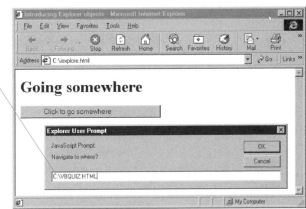

A Web location is called a URL, which stands for Uniform Resource Locator. This can be a file as well as a Web location, but only if you are running the browser on the same network as the file.

4 This script opens a new Explorer Window at a chosen location:

```
Sub cbOpenWindow_OnClick
window.open  "C:\VBQUIZ.HTML","MyNewWin"
End Sub
```

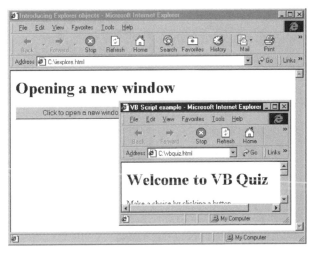

Introducing Dynamic HTML

Versions of Microsoft Internet Explorer after and including 4.0 use Dynamic HTML, a significant advance over the HTML standard in Internet Explorer 3.0. The reason is that in Dynamic HTML a Web page has a Document Object Model, which means that every element can be identified and scripted.

The following example shows one way of using Visual Basic to change the text of a Web page dynamically. It uses the <SPAN> tag to identify a section of text with a name. This makes that section of text a programmable object. The code writes to the innerHTML property of this object, and in doing so changes the text. There is also an innerText property, but the advantage of innerHTML is that you can include formatting as well as text.

A Dynamic Text example

This example displays a new quote when you click the button:

I Including text within the <SPAN> tag makes this part of the document into an object that you can use in your script.

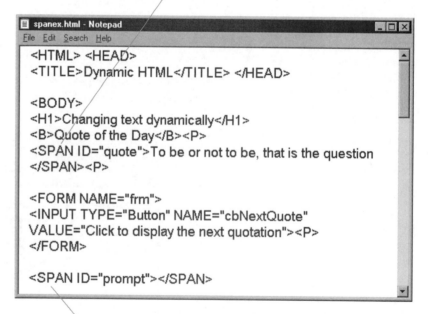

```
spanex.html - Notepad
File  Edit  Search  Help

<HTML> <HEAD>
<TITLE>Dynamic HTML</TITLE> </HEAD>

<BODY>
<H1>Changing text dynamically</H1>
<B>Quote of the Day</B><P>
<SPAN ID="quote">To be or not to be, that is the question
</SPAN><P>

<FORM NAME="frm">
<INPUT TYPE="Button" NAME="cbNextQuote"
VALUE="Click to display the next quotation"><P>
</FORM>

<SPAN ID="prompt"></SPAN>
```

2 This second <SPAN> section has no text at all when the page first loads.

...cont'd

Dynamic HTML is complex, but there is a complete reference in Visual Basic's online Help.

3 This script has a script level variable to let you cycle through quotes. The OnClick procedure shows the quote that matches the number, and then increases the

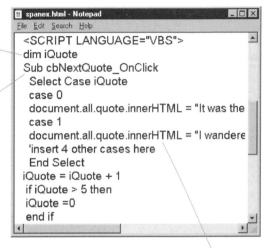

```
spanex.html - Notepad
File  Edit  Search  Help
<SCRIPT LANGUAGE="VBS">
dim iQuote
Sub cbNextQuote_OnClick
  Select Case iQuote
  case 0
  document.all.quote.innerHTML = "It was the
  case 1
  document.all.quote.innerHTML = "I wandere
  'insert 4 other cases here
  End Select
iQuote = iQuote + 1
if iQuote > 5 then
iQuote =0
end if
```

number or resets it to zero. The quote is displayed by setting the innerHTML property of the <SPAN> object.

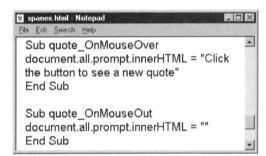

```
spanex.html - Notepad
File  Edit  Search  Help
Sub quote_OnMouseOver
document.all.prompt.innerHTML = "Click
the button to see a new quote"
End Sub

Sub quote_OnMouseOut
document.all.prompt.innerHTML = ""
End Sub
```

4 This code displays a prompt when the mouse is over a quotation and removes it when it moves.

You can also display tooltips in a Web page, by giving objects a TITLE attribute.

5 Test your work by opening the page in Internet Explorer. Click the button to show a new quote. Move the mouse to show the prompt.

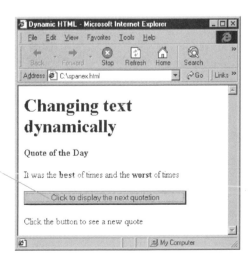

Dynamic HTML - Microsoft Internet Explorer
File Edit View Favorites Tools Help
Address C:\spanex.html

Changing text dynamically

Quote of the Day

It was the **best** of times and the **worst** of times

[Click to display the next quotation]

Click the button to see a new quote

Using a Web timer for animation

The most dynamic Web pages are those which are active even when the user is not clicking the mouse. You can easily achieve this using Internet Explorer's built-in timer.

The one thing to be careful about is that the timer procedure must not take too long to execute. If you loaded large graphic files, for example, the effect would be frustrating rather than impressive.

The way it works is that when the page loads, you call the browser window's SetInterval method, passing the name of another procedure as the parameter, along with a time interval in milliseconds. The timer then calls that procedure repeatedly, at the requested time interval. In your procedure you can load images, create text effects, in fact do anything that VB Script allows.

A timer example

This script is quite similar to the one on the previous page, so not all of it is shown.

Use <SPAN> to set up a text object. This will contain a changing message. Note the use of the FONT SIZE tag to obtain a large font.

```
<FONT SIZE="+6"><SPAN
ID="dynText"></SPAN><P></FONT>
```

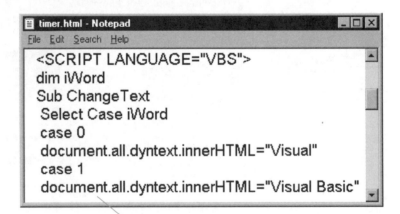

```
<SCRIPT LANGUAGE="VBS">
dim iWord
Sub ChangeText
 Select Case iWord
 case 0
 document.all.dyntext.innerHTML="Visual"
 case 1
 document.all.dyntext.innerHTML="Visual Basic"
```

2 Write a ChangeText procedure which changes the text each time it is called. This example gradually reveals a message. Note the use once again of a script level variable.

Adjust the second parameter to change the speed at which the message displays.

3 This is the key bit of code. When the document loads, this event fires, calling the SetInterval function. The first parameter is the name of your ChangeText procedure. The second is the number of milliseconds between calls.

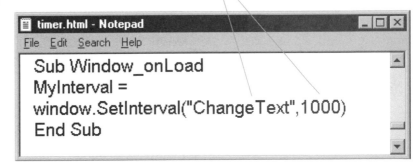

```
Sub Window_onLoad
MyInterval =
window.SetInterval("ChangeText",1000)
End Sub
```

A snag with animated text is that it can be distracting or irritating. It is a good idea to reserve this kind of effect for pages which do not require concentration! You can be sure your message will be noticed.

4 Load the page in Internet Explorer to see the results. The message builds up gradually, starting the cycle again when it is complete, for a truly dynamic effect:

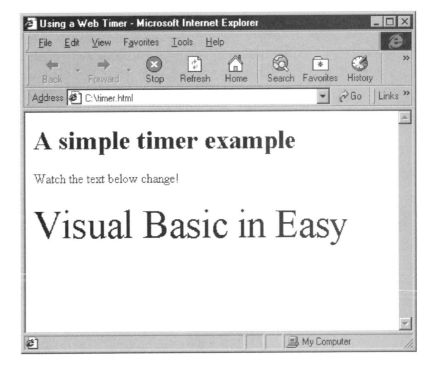

A simple timer example

Watch the text below change!

Visual Basic in Easy

Introducing Web Forms

A Web Form is the same as an ASP .Net page. In order to use Web Forms, you must have a Windows Web server on your network, that has the .NET Framework installed. You can install this on your own machine, and it is an option in the Visual Studio setup. Alternatively, if you are on an Intranet, there may be a Web server elsewhere on the network that you can use. For full Visual Studio support, there are other special requirements such as the FrontPage extensions. Permissions also have to be configured correctly to support ASP .Net debugging. If you are installing on your own machine, the Visual Studio setup will configure the server for you.

Having a Web server installed can be a security risk when you dial the Internet. Check Microsoft's website for the latest security information about Internet Information Server.

A word about deployment

If you want to do more than just experiment with Web forms, you will want to deploy your work. On an Intranet that is no problem. If you want to publish to the Web, then you need an ISP that supports the .Net Framework (unless you are lucky enough to have your own Web server permanently connected and open to the Internet). Some ISPs charge extra for ASP .Net services, while others may not support it at all.

Visual Studio's Start page has a list of ASP .Net providers. Some of these allow free accounts, sometimes on a temporary basis, so you can try out their services. It doesn't matter if the ISP is in a different country from your own. If the ISP is happy for you to have an account with them, there is no technical problem. Connection speed is likely to be a little slower than with a local ISP.

If you lose the Start page, you can display it from the Help menu.

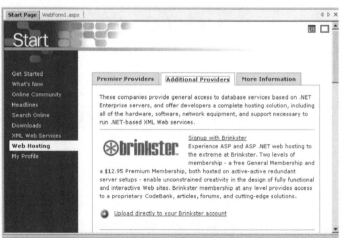

Providers listed in the Visual Studio Start page

Creating a Web Form

1. From the File menu, choose New Project and select ASP .Net Web Application. In the Location box, type:

    ```
    http://
    localhost/
    EasyWeb
    ```

    Then click OK.

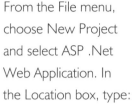 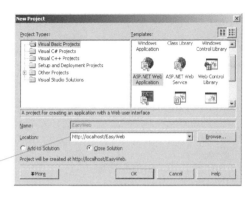

2. You will see this dialog while Visual Basic creates the necessary files on the Web server.

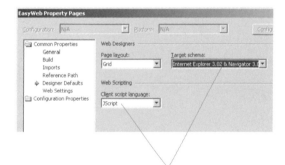

3. Open the Solution Explorer, right-click the name of the project and choose Properties. Right

at the beginning, it is important to set the Target Schema. If you are targeting the public Web, normally choose the Internet Explorer 3.02 and Navigator 3.0 option. If you are targeting an Intranet or just learning ASP .Net, it is fine to choose Internet Explorer 5.0. Leave the client script at JScript for the Web, and normally also for Intranets unless you have a good reason to use VB Script. In ASP .Net, most of the client script is generated for you, so it does not matter if you don't know JScript.

4 Select the Web Forms section of the Toolbox and drag a Label, a TextBox and a Button to the form.

The HTML view of a Web form lets you edit the HTML source that makes up the Web page. Any changes you make are reflected in the design view as well. It is often best to let Visual Basic generate most of the HTML, but some changes have to be made manually.

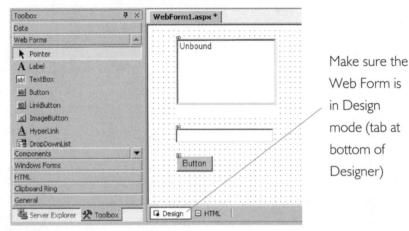

Make sure the Web Form is in Design mode (tab at bottom of Designer)

5 Select the Button and press F4 to display its properties. Set the Text property to Add item.

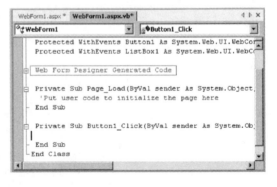

A code-behind file is a Visual Basic class that is linked to the Web page. In practice, it works in the same way as the code view of a Windows form.

6 Double-click the button to open its Click event handler. There will be a pause while Visual Basic creates a "code-behind" file. Then the code editor opens.

7 Here is the code for the Click event handler:

```
Dim s As String = Trim(TextBox1.Text)
If s <> "" Then
   ListBox1.Items.Add(s)
End If
TextBox1.Text = ""
```

8 Return to the Design view, click on a blank part of the Web Form and press F4. The Properties Explorer should say DOCUMENT; if it does not, select DOCUMENT from the drop-down list. Here you can amend the properties of the page. Change the Title to Web Pages in Easy Steps.

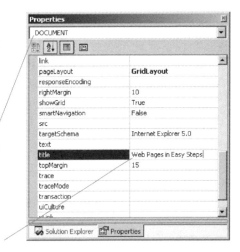

9 Run the project. Enter some text in the text box and click Add item. The text you type appears in the list. Note that the title of the page appears in the browser. An interesting thing to do is to right-click the page in the browser and choose Visual Source. There is

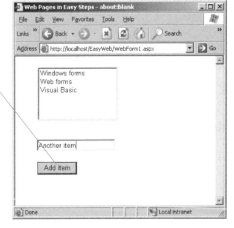

no script visible. When you click the button, the page is fetched afresh from the Web server. All the code runs on the server.

How Web Forms work

Although it is a simple application, the Web Form you have constructed has some advanced features:

- It runs full Visual Basic code, not just script code

- When you add an item to the list, the items that were previously added remain as well. Normally, when you refresh a Web page, any information you enter is lost

- Coding the Web Form is very similar to coding a Windows form

How it works

The code behind a Visual Basic Web Form application is compiled to a .Net Framework library. When the page is requested by a browser, the Web server reads the Web page (normally with an .aspx extension) and interprets any special tags. In addition, it fires events that are handled by the code-behind class, and which can modify the contents of the page that gets returned to the browser.

Managing state

If you look at the source of an ASP .Net page in the browser (not the source in Visual Basic), you can see the VIEWSTATE field. It is plain text and does not require any special browser features. It can be quite large, and some Web forms are optimised by reducing the use of VIEWSTATE.

In addition, the page has a hidden field called VIEWSTATE. The current value of the controls on the page is encoded into this field. When the user clicks a button on the form, the Web server is able to read back the previous state of the controls on the page through VIEWSTATE. ASP .Net generates a new version of the page incorporating both the VIEWSTATE values and any new changes. This way, there could be dozens of users using the site at the same time, each one adding different values to the list, and each user will get their own list back from the Web server.

For success with Web Forms, it is important to remember that although you can code them in a similar way to Windows forms, state is managed in this different way. In addition, there is a feature called Session state, that lets you store variables linked to the current user. Other than through special techniques like these, objects do not retain their values between page requests. After all, the next page request might be for a different user.

The Web Forms Toolbox

When working with Web Forms, there are three sections on the Toolbox that you will use most frequently:

The **Web Forms section** is for rich ASP .Net controls. These range from simple objects like labels and TextBoxes, through to advanced controls like the calendars and the DataGrid. These controls must run on the Web server. You can write code against them in the same way as for Windows Form controls

Why not run all HTML controls at the server? The reason is that this is a little slower. If you don't need program control, a plain HTML control is the fastest option.

The **HTML section** is for standard HTML controls, but with an important difference. You can design a Web page visually with these controls, in the same way as with other Web design tools like FrontPage. The difference is that by right-clicking one of these controls and choosing Run as server control, you can handle events and code their properties just as for Web Form controls

One of the best features of ASP .Net is easy access to data. The **Data Section** is applicable to Web Forms just as it is to Windows Forms

Showing data in a datagrid

1 Start a new ASP .Net project and call it EasyData. Set the TargetSchema as shown on page 151. Then place a DataGrid on the form.

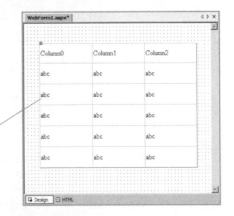

2 If you followed the Sports Club example on page 117, you will have the connection to sports.mdb in the Server Explorer. If not, follow the procedures there to create it, or a connection to another database. Drag the Members table to the form. It will create two new objects, OleDbConnection1 and OleDbDataAdapter1.

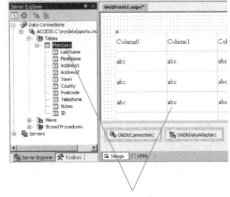

3 Right-click the DataAdapter and open the Configuration Wizard by selecting Configure Data Adapter. Select the existing data connection. In the SQL Select field, type:

SELECT FirstName, LastName, Town, Telephone, ID FROM Members ORDER BY LastName, FirstName

Accept the other defaults and close the Wizard.

If you prefer you can use the Query Builder as on page 127.

...cont'd

4 Right-click the
DataAdapter and choose
Generate Dataset. Call
the Dataset dsMembers.
Then close with OK.

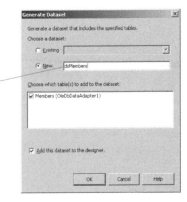

*This application
makes no use
of the Data key
field. It is useful
when you want
to get the primary key of a
record from a row in the
DataGrid, without having to
display the key.*

5 It is now possible to
configure the
DataGrid. Right-click
the control and
choose Property
Builder. On the
General tab, set
DataSource to
DsMembers1,
DataMember to
Members, and
DataKeyField to ID.

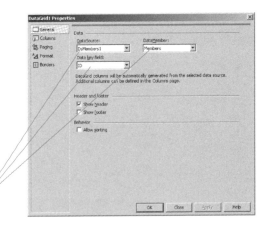

*If you have
columns
generated
automatically,
it is inflexible.
In addition, you can easily
end up with some columns
repeated.*

6 Next, click the
Columns section.
Uncheck the option to
Create columns
automatically at run
time. Then select all the
columns except ID. For
FirstName and
LastName, change the
Header text to add a
space between the words.

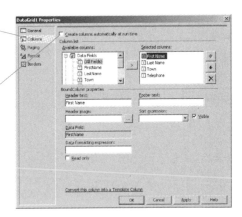

The DataGrid is a rich control with many formatting options. You can also display fields in the form of other controls such as checkboxes or images.

7 Next, select the Format section. Click Header and check Bold.

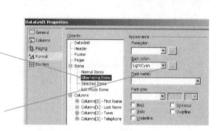

8 Expand the Items section and select Alternating Items. Click Back color and select a light colour for the background of alternate rows.

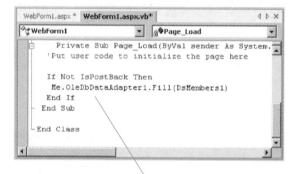

9 Close the Property Builder and double-click the Web Form to open the code-behind at the Page Load event handler. Add the code shown.

If you get an error stating that the database is in use or cannot be accessed, it is most likely a permissions issue. The user account used by ASP .Net must be able to read and write data to the folder where the Access database is located. This account is sometimes called ASPNET.

10 Run the application. Here, a label has been added to the form to make a heading. This is live data from the Access database; if the data is modified, the page will change next time it is refreshed.

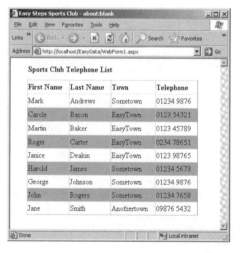

Tips for Experts

Creating Visual Basic applications is one thing; creating good ones another. This chapter explains error-trapping and offers many tips for building applications that work reliably and fast.

Covers

Chapter Eight

Introducing error-trapping

Visual Basic is safer for the user than many alternative programming systems. A Visual Basic application is unlikely to cause your system to crash, for example. However, there are still plenty of reasons why errors occur. Most are caused by errors in your code, or by failing to anticipate all the ways in which your program may be used. Here is a simple example:

Users may not know what to make of dialogs like this one. Wherever possible, it is better to anticipate errors and deal with them in code.

Hitting an error in Visual Basic

You can see the reason for the error if you see the code:

```
Dim iNumOne As Integer
   Dim iNumTwo As Integer
   iNumOne = Val(TextBox1.Text)
   iNumTwo = Val(TextBox2.Text)
   Label1.Text = "The result is: " & Str(iNumOne +
iNumTwo)
```

The variables iNumOne and iNumTwo are declared as integers. This works fine with small numbers, but if the result is above 2,147,483,648 the application stops with an overflow error. Even if you DIM these variables as Long, it is easy to enter a number large enough to cause an overflow.

Exceptions

Errors like these are called Exceptions, because they are regarded as exceptional circumstances. There are two main techniques for preventing them:

- Validation, to prevent the exceptional circumstance from occurring

- Exception handling, to deal cleanly with exceptions that occur

Here is how to improve the last example by adding an exception handler:

The term "exception-handler" means a section of code which only runs when an exception has occurred. Its purpose is to recover gracefully from the problem.

This line sets up the exception-handler

This line starts a block of code that only runs when an exception has occurred

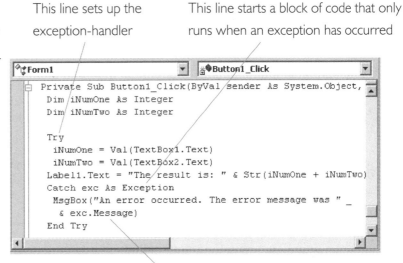

```
Form1                              Button1_Click
  Private Sub Button1_Click(ByVal sender As System.Object,
    Dim iNumOne As Integer
    Dim iNumTwo As Integer

    Try
      iNumOne = Val(TextBox1.Text)
      iNumTwo = Val(TextBox2.Text)
    Label1.Text = "The result is: " & Str(iNumOne + iNumTwo)
    Catch exc As Exception
      MsgBox("An error occurred. The error message was " _
        & exc.Message)
    End Try
```

By checking the message property of the Exception object, an appropriate message is displayed

Trying out the Exception handler

Here is what happens when you run the new code:

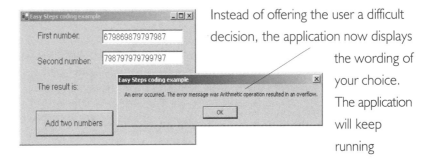

Instead of offering the user a difficult decision, the application now displays the wording of your choice. The application will keep running

See the next page for a better exception-handler.

Even this is not an excellent exception handler. It does not tell the user in plain English why the error has occurred. Because it is a universal exception handler, the programmer cannot really know what message to display, and has to resort to the Message property of the Exception object. Therefore, the best code looks for likely exceptions and deals with them individually.

A better exception handler

Visual Basic, or more accurately the .NET Framework, has numerous Exception classes which inherit from the base Exception class. There are two ways you can exploit this. You can inspect the Exception in a generic exception handler with code like:

```
If TypeOf (exc) Is OverflowException Then
```

Alternatively, you can have multiple Catch statements:

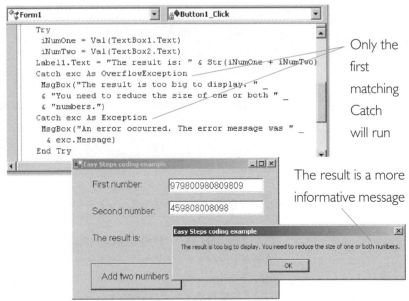

Only the first matching Catch will run

The result is a more informative message

This message could be further improved by adding code, for example to check which number was too large. Good error messages are clear, avoid technical language, and explain what the user needs to do next. It can also be helpful to include a telephone number for technical support.

If you have multiple Catch statements, they must be ordered from the most specific to the least specific, as once a matching Catch statement is found, no others will run. You can check the hierarchy in online Help. For example, OverFlowException inherits from ArithmeticException. Therefore, you could look first for an OverFlowException, next for an ArithmeticException, and last for a generic Exception.

You can also use Catch on its own, without including an Exception variable. This will catch any error, but it's more convenient to include a reference to the Exception object. If necessary, you can get at the current exception through the global Err object:

```
Dim exc as Exception = Err.GetException()
```

Try... Finally

A great feature of Visual Basic is that the Try code block can also include a Finally clause. Code following the Finally statement always runs, whether or not there was an exception. Finally can be combined with Catch, as a Try... Catch... Finally block, or you can use it on its own as Try... Finally.

Here is an example:

The Finally block can save a lot of conditional code. Use it for code that must always be executed, for example to clean up resources.

```
Dim sr As StreamReader
'Read a log file and display lines beginning "Error"
Try ' try to open the file
 sr = File.OpenText("c:\MyData\MyLog.txt")
 Try ' try to read the file
  Dim s As String, l As String
   While sr.Peek <> -1
   l = sr.ReadLine()
    If Strings.Left(l, 5) = "Error" Then
    s += l
    End If
   End While
  TextBox1.Text = s
 Finally
 'Always close the file
  sr.Close()
 End Try
Catch exc As Exception
MsgBox("There was an error: " & exc.Message)
End Try
```

File handling is prone to errors. The file might not exist, or it might be opened exclusively by another application, or it may contain unexpected characters. In the above example, the first Try block is focused on opening the file. If the code gets as far as the second Try statement, then the file is open and a Finally clause is used to ensure that it is closed. It is no good using a single Try block, since if the file was not opened, attempting to close it then will itself raise an exception. A nested block like this deals with both the possibilities.

Using validation

Validation is about making sure input is correct before attempting an operation. Although exception handling is a great way out of trouble, it is better to detect and prevent the problem before it reaches an exception handler.

The Validating event

Many Visual Basic controls have a Validating event that you can use to check data input. Here is an example:

This code checks the size of the number. If it is too large, then the Cancel property is set to True, ensuring that the user cannot continue without fixing the problem.

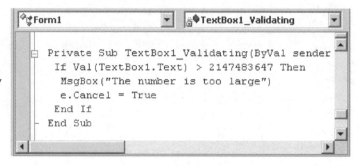

```
Private Sub TextBox1_Validating(ByVal sender
   If Val(TextBox1.Text) > 2147483647 Then
     MsgBox("The number is too large")
     e.Cancel = True
   End If
 End Sub
```

To handle the Validating event, first find the control in the left-hand dropdown list, and then select the Validating event from the right-hand dropdown list.

When the code runs, the user is prompted that the number is too large. The Validating event runs as soon as the focus leaves the TextBox

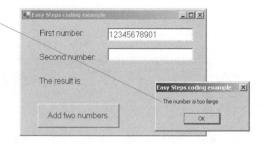

Validation can take many different forms. It does not have to be done in a Validating event. Sometimes validating code needs to look up values in a database or refer to the value of other fields on a form. It is always important to think about the user's experience. That means giving a simple, clear and polite explanation of what is wrong and making it easy to fix. For example, a message that simply reported "Invalid number" would be irritating not helpful.

Trapping the user

The above example leaves the user trapped on the TextBox until a valid number is entered. It would be better still to offer an escape option, say to clear the form, so the user does not feel hemmed in by the application.

Helping the user

One of the best ways to avoid errors is by making it hard for the user to make mistakes.

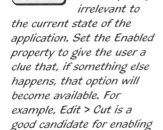

Set the Visible property for options that are completely irrelevant to the current state of the application. Set the Enabled property to give the user a clue that, if something else happens, that option will become available. For example, Edit > Cut is a good candidate for enabling and disabling rather than hiding completely.

1. Use the Enabled and Visible properties

Most applications have buttons and menu options which are not always relevant. Worse, if used at the wrong moment they might cause an error. For example, you might have a Close option which closes a document. If there is no document open, Close means nothing.

The solution is to either hide or disable irrelevant or dangerous options. In your Open code, you could have a line like this:

```
mnuFileClose.Enabled = True
```

When the last document is closed, you can have:

```
mnuFileClose.Enabled = False
```

If you prefer to remove the option completely, use the Visible property.

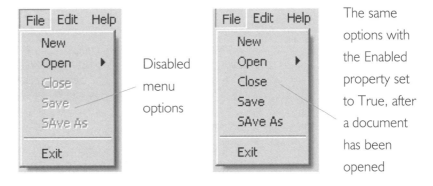

Disabled menu options

The same options with the Enabled property set to True, after a document has been opened

To change the shape of the mouse-pointer, set the Cursor property for a form or a control. See online Help for the possible values, which include Cursors.Waitcursor and Cursors.Arrow.

2. Use ToolTips, progress bars and status bars

Instant Help text that appears when an option is selected, or when the mouse is over a control, is a very useful to the user. See the next page for how to show ToolTips.

If an operation takes a significant amount of time, set the mouse pointer to an hourglass and show progress in a status bar or progress bar whenever possible. Users need to see something happening, in case they assume the application has crashed.

How to use ToolTips

The ToolTip control has its own properties, which determine whether ToolTips are active, how long it takes for them to pop-up, and how long they stay visible once shown.

1 Drag the ToolTip control to a form. It appears as an icon in the area below the form.

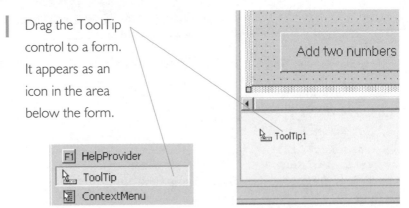

2 Select a control on the form, such as a button, and set the "ToolTip on ToolTip1" property to a help text of your choice.

3 Run the project, and hover the mouse over the button to see the ToolTip.

You can also set ToolTip properties in code. The advantage would be that you could vary the ToolTip according to the state of the application. For example, a disabled button could have a ToolTip giving the reason why the button is disabled. When enabled, it could explain what the button does. If you set a ToolTip in code and also in the Properties window, the code will override the property setting.

There is no problem with using the same ToolTip control for more than one control. It represents a convenient way to make settings that affect all the ToolTips on a form.

How to organise your code

As soon as your applications are more than trivial, you will need to think carefully about how to organise your code. One question is when to use a function or procedure. User-defined functions and procedures have the effect of breaking up your code into smaller chunks. There are three main reasons to use them:

If you ever find yourself copying and pasting code, ask yourself whether it would be better to create a function, subroutine or class to handle the processing. Copied code is a common source of bugs.

- When you would otherwise repeat the same section of code at several points in your application. If you are tempted to copy and paste code from another part of the project, consider using a function or procedure instead. Repeated code is error-prone, since you might later on amend one copy of the code but not the other

- To avoid long blocks of code. Longer blocks of code are harder to read and therefore more error-prone

- To make it easier to maintain and improve the code. For example, imagine you have a charting feature that draws a chart, called by both a menu option and a toolbar button. You could put all the code in the Click event for both these controls, but that is inefficient, and worse still, you might make changes to one but forget to make the same changes in the other. It is better to have a DrawChart procedure which you can call from both Click events. DrawChart could be in the general section of a form, or better still in a separate class. If you later want to improve the chart-drawing code, you will know exactly where to find it in the project

One advantage of using separate classes is that you can build up a library, which you can use in many different projects.

The keyword Call is optional, but it can be useful to clarify that the code is calling a subroutine rather than a built-in function. If you invoke a function with Call, the return value is ignored.

This has all the code in one Click procedure

Here, the real work has moved to a separate procedure, called from the Click event handler

Tips for readable code

When you are enthusiastic about a project, it is easy to bang out lines and lines of code. Later on, when you come to correct or improve the code, it is important to be able to find your way around easily. Here are some tips:

1. Use plenty of white space

The names you choose for functions, procedures and variables also make a difference to readability. See the next page for some tips.

When Visual Basic runs your project, the white space, in the form of blank lines and indents, is ignored. You can take advantage of that by using it generously in your code. Separate your functions into logical blocks and use one or two blank lines between them.

2. Indent carefully

Indentation is even more important. It is easy to get confused by long, multi-level If or Select Case blocks. Make a point of indenting each new level in a consistent way throughout your code.

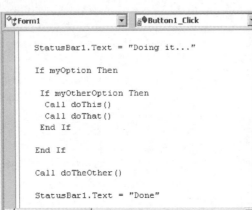

```
Form1                       Button1_Click

    StatusBar1.Text = "Doing it..."

    If myOption Then

     If myOtherOption Then
      Call doThis()
      Call doThat()
     End If

    End If

    Call doTheOther()

    StatusBar1.Text = "Done"
```

Use blank lines and indentation to make it easy to see the structure of If blocks. Visual Basic makes this easy with auto formatting

Any line that begins with a single quote mark is a comment. You can also add comments to the end of a line, following a single quote character.

3. Comment generously

Like white space, comments are ignored at runtime so they do not slow down your code.

Ideally, comment each function and procedure to show what they do. If you are working in a team, show when they were written, and who by, and when last amended. If there are parameters, say what they are for.

If you add some code to work around a problem, add a comment to explain why that code was added. Otherwise, you or someone else may come along later, not know why it is there, and delete it.

Choosing descriptive names

The names you choose for functions, procedures and variables make no difference at runtime. They do, however, make a difference to the readability of your code. Professional programmers have been known to deliberately obscure their code, simply by changing all the names to meaningless ones. More often, though, programmers want to make code easy to understand.

1. Use descriptive names

It is better to have names that are descriptive rather than short. Better to have a function called:

```
GetIncomeFromEmployeeId(EmployeeID as Integer)
```

than this concise alternative:

```
GetInc(ID as Integer)
```

2. Use a naming convention

Visual Basic is not case-sensitive, but you can make good use of upper and lower case in the names you choose.

Programmers love to argue about what is the best way to choose names. Schemes for devising names are called naming conventions. For example, it is useful to identify the type of an object or variable by using a consistent prefix, e.g.:

strSomething	For a string
iSomething	For an integer
sglSomething	For a single
txtSomething	For a text box

The advantage of this approach is that you are less likely to try things that cause errors, like storing a floating-point number in an integer variable.

In this book, the examples often use the default Visual Basic names for controls, like Button1 and Label1. This is to help beginners put together short examples; it is not good practice in real programming work. You will have lots of forms with controls called Button1 and Label1, and tracing through the code will not be easy.

Tips for fast applications

However fast your PC, it is still worth considering your application's performance, especially if you distribute your work to others, since some will have slow systems. Here are some key tips:

1. Declare all variables

Use Option Explicit to ensure that all variables are declared. Check the Build section in Project Properties.

Variables which are not declared As a type are invisibly declared as Objects by Visual Basic. Objects are slower to process than other kinds of variable. The single most important thing you can do to speed up projects is to Dim all variables As the appropriate type.

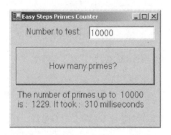

This little application calculates prime numbers. It runs at nearly six times the speed of the one below

Where you can, use integers rather than floating-point numbers.
Integers are faster for the computer to process. Integers are also faster than Long integers.

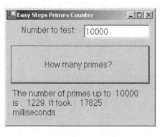

The code is identical in both, except that in this slow version the variables are declared without using As

2. Minimise usage of COM interop

Speed is not the only factor. Productivity counts as well. Sometimes getting reliable code written quickly is more important than performance.

Using COM components such as ActiveX controls may slow down an application. Another problem is that larger ActiveX controls probably have more features than you need. To keep your application slim and fast, only use ActiveX controls when you really need them.

3. Exceptions are slow

Code that raises many exceptions will be slow, even if they are correctly handled. Try ... Catch blocks are not inherently slow, but only when the exceptions are actually thrown.

4. Value types are faster than objects

Types like Integers and Structures perform better than objects.

Managing multiple forms

Most of the examples in this book have only used one form. To build a complete application, you will often find that you need more than one form. Here is how you include additional forms in your project:

1 From the File menu, choose Add New Item.

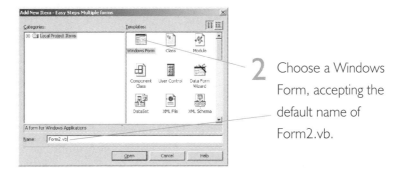

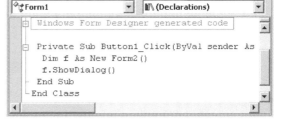

2 Choose a Windows Form, accepting the default name of Form2.vb.

Should you close a form with Hide or Close? Although both close a form, they do different things. Hide leaves the form in memory, so it is good if you need to refer to the values of its controls, or will be displaying it again soon. Close removes the form from memory and is good if you want to conserve system resources.

3 The new form is a class. To use it in your code, first declare an object of that class, and then call its Show() method. If you want to use the form as a modal dialog, which must be closed before the user continues with anything else, call ShowDialog() instead.

```
Form1                    (Declarations)
   Windows Form Designer generated code

   Private Sub Button1_Click(ByVal sender As
      Dim f As New Form2()
      f.ShowDialog()
   End Sub
End Class
```

4 You can close the form at runtime either by allowing the user to click the Close button at top-right, or in code with the Close() method. If you want the form to persist after it is closed, close it with Hide() and keep the object variable in scope so you can show it again.

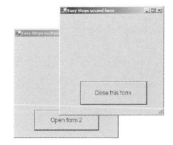

Introducing MDI

Applications which use multiple forms can get untidy, especially if the forms are displayed non-modally. If there are several applications open, it can even be hard to tell which form belongs to which application.

MDI stands for Multiple Document Interface. It is a way of managing multiple windows by trapping them within a master window. In Visual Basic, this master window is called a MDI form. Then, forms can be displayed as MDI children, which can be moved within the master form, but not outside it. Most word-processors and spreadsheets are MDI applications.

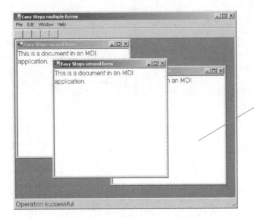

A MDI application encloses one or more forms. It is typically used for applications that handle documents, such as word processors

MDI forms have a property called ActiveMdiChild, which gives you a reference to the child form that currently has the focus. This enables you to target code to the correct form.

Working with MDI forms

There is not enough space here for a full description of MDI. Getting started is easy, though. First, begin a new application. Then set the main form's IsMdiContainer property to True. Finally, when you create a child form, set its MdiParent property to the MDI container form. For example, if you were opening the child form from a button or menu on the main form, you could write:

```
f = New Form2()
f.MdiParent = Me
f.Show()
```

MDI forms have some special features. A menu can be set to MDIList, which means it shows a list of open windows and activates the one selected. This is important, especially if a document is maximized.

Using Sub Main

All Visual Basic projects have a startup object. This determines which code runs first when the project opens. The startup object is set in Project Properties, and can either be one of the forms in the project (by default it is the first form), or else a procedure with the special name of Sub Main.

Click here to set Sub Main
instead of a startup form

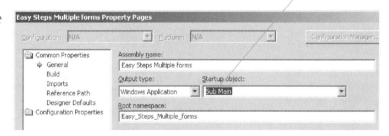

Why use Sub Main?

In an application which is more than trivial, using Sub Main has several advantages. It is a convenient place to set variables to default values, open a database, or check that all the files needed by the application exist. Then you can display the initial form using its ShowDialog() method.

Including a splash screen

Starting with Sub Main makes it easy to display a splash screen. This is a form which shows while your application starts up. If the full application takes a while to load, the splash screen reassures the user that all is well. Simply include a line like:

```
frmSplash.show
Application.DoEvents()
' allows the form to be painted
```

at the beginning of Sub Main. When you have done all the initialisation, continue with

```
frmSplash.close()
frmMain.showDialog()
```

How to read and write to a file

Most real-world applications need to read and write disk files. In many cases this is done for you behind the scenes. For example, if you use Visual Basic's database features, then the disk access is handled by the database engine. You do not need to worry about opening or closing disk files directly.

Even so, knowing how to read and write information on a disk is a valuable skill. For example, you might want to write and display a log file. This sample shows how you can write out a text file and then load it into a window:

Importing the Namespace for System.IO saves you having to add the statement to the top of each Visual Basic file where you want to use the IO library. IO stands for Input/Output.

1 Start a new project and open its properties (right-click the project name in Solution Explorer). In the Imports section, type System.IO in the Namespace box and click Add import.

2 On the project's main form, add a TextBox with its Multiline property set to True, and a button.

If you develop this project, a good plan would be to give WriteFile a parameter so that you could pass it a line of text to write.

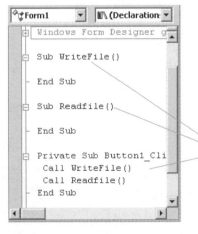

3 Double-click the button to open its Click event handler. Before writing any code, scroll up in the editor and create two Subs, WriteFile and ReadFile. Then add the code shown to the Click event handler.

4 Now add the code for the two Subs. Here it is:

```
Sub WriteFile()
Dim sw As StreamWriter
Try
 sw = New _
 StreamWriter(File.Open _
 ("C:\EasyLog.txt", FileMode.OpenOrCreate))
 Try
  sw.BaseStream.Seek(0, SeekOrigin.End)
  sw.WriteLine("Log entry added at: " &_
  Now.ToShortTimeString)
  sw.Flush()
 Finally
 sw.Close()
 End Try
Catch exc As Exception
 TextBox1.Text = "Error: " & exc.Message
End Try
End Sub
```

This example does not teach you all you need to know about reading and writing files. It does, however, show how easy it is to get started.

```
Sub Readfile()
Dim sr As StreamReader
Dim s As String
Try
 sr = New _
 StreamReader(File.Open _
 ("C:\EasyLog.txt", FileMode.Open))
 Try
  TextBox1.Text = sr.ReadToEnd
 Finally
  sr.Close()
 End Try
Catch exc As Exception
 TextBox1.Text = exc.Message
End Try
End Sub
```

This is how the code works. StreamWriter and StreamReader are objects that know how to write and read text files (not binary files). The File object's Open method returns a FileStream object, which is used to create the StreamWriter and StreamReader objects. The StreamWriter seeks to the end of the file and writes a line, then Flush is called to make sure it is actually written to disk, and finally it is closed.

The StreamReader has a convenient ReadToEnd method that reads the entire contents of a file into a String, which becomes the Text property of the TextBox.

5 Run the project and click the button several times to add entries to the log.

```
Easy Steps file handling          _ □ ×
Log entry added at: 20:05
Log entry added at: 20:06
Log entry added at: 20:06
Log entry added at: 20:06
Log entry added at: 20:06
Log entry added at: 20:06
Log entry added at: 20:07



              Write and show the file
```

Drawing graphics

Users rightly expect Windows applications to display information graphically. Using Visual Basic's graphic methods, you can draw your own charts and graphs on forms and picture boxes.

How to draw in a PictureBox

So is there an even easier way to draw a chart or graph? One way is to use a third-party chart component, so you could avoid the lower-level graphics functions.

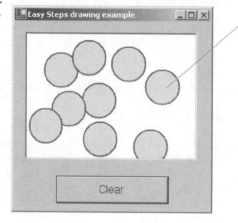

This example uses a form, a PictureBox and a button. Each time the mouse clicks on the PictureBox, a filled circle is drawn where the mouse lands.

See the next page for more information on how this code works.

2 Place the following code in the PictureBox's MouseDown event handler:

```
Dim g As Graphics
'create a bitmap to persist the drawing
If PictureBox1.Image Is Nothing Then
 Dim bm As New _
   Bitmap(PictureBox1.ClientSize.Width, _
   PictureBox1.ClientSize.Height)
   PictureBox1.Image = bm
End If
'get a graphics object
g = Graphics.FromImage(PictureBox1.Image)
Dim br As New SolidBrush(Color.Yellow)
Dim pn As New Drawing.Pen(System.Drawing.Color.Red, 2)
g.DrawEllipse(pn, e.X - 25, e.Y - 25, 50, 50)
g.FillEllipse(br, New RectangleF _
(e.X - 24, e.Y - 24, 48, 48))
' clean up
pn.Dispose()
br.Dispose()
g.Dispose()
'repaint the picturebox
PictureBox1.Refresh()
```

3 The code for clearing the PictureBox is short:

```
If Not PictureBox1.Image Is Nothing Then
   PictureBox1.Image.Dispose()
   PictureBox1.Image = Nothing
End If
PictureBox1.Image = Nothing
```

How this code works

Visual Basic does not have any simple graphical controls like lines or shapes. Instead, you draw on a control surface using graphical methods. The code shown uses several objects:

Graphics: Provides methods for drawing to a surface.

Bitmap: An object representing a bitmap image.

Pen: An object that controls how lines are drawn.

Brush: An object that controls how fills are drawn.

It is possible to draw on a PictureBox without creating a bitmap, but such drawings will by default disappear whenever the control has to be repainted, for example if it is covered by another window and then uncovered. The Bitmap object persists the image. Therefore, the code creates a bitmap in memory and draws on that. The PictureBox does not automatically repaint itself when the bitmap changes, so the code calls its Refresh() method to force a repaint.

Objects like Graphics, Bitmap, Pen and Brush use system resources. These objects have a Dispose method that you should call once you have finished with them, to free these resources.

The Graphics classes are based on a Windows API (Application Programming Interface) called GDI+. Although this code is a little more difficult than most Visual Basic code, GDI+ is a powerful API with many options for textured, transparent, blended and gradated drawing that can produce some highly sophisticated effects. You can also use text in creative ways.

Creating a shared event handler

Sometimes you will find that several buttons or other controls need to run identical code. Using Visual Basic, you can have one event handler respond to the events from more than one control. This is similar to what was achieved in Visual Basic 6.0 and earlier using a Control Array. The following example shows how you might use this technique to have a search button for each letter of the alphabet (although only the first four letters are implemented here):

1 Place a Button on a form, size it small, and choose Edit>Copy. Then choose Edit>Paste. Place three more similar copies on a form.

2 Name the buttons BtnA, BtnB, BtnC and BtnD. Give them Text properties of A, B, C and D in turn.

3 Now double-click BtnA to open its Click event handler. In order to handle the Click events for the other buttons as well, extend the Handles clause with a comma-separated list of events. The rest of the code is designed to extend the example beginning on page 125. When you run the code, clicking a button retrieves all the lastnames beginning with the letter on the Button.

In this code, notice how the sender object is assigned to a Button variable, in order to read off the Text property of each Button. For this to work, you must ensure that the code only handles Button events.

```
Private Sub btnA_Click(ByVal sender As System.Object, _
ByVal e As System.EventArgs) _
Handles btnA.Click, btnB.Click, btnC.Click, btnD.Click
Dim btn As Button = sender
Dim search As String = "'" & btn.Text & "%'"
DsMembers1.Clear()
OleDbDataAdapter1.SelectCommand.CommandText = _
"SELECT FirstName, LastName, Address1, Address2," _
& "Town, County, Postcode, Telephone, ID " & _
"FROM Members WHERE LastName Like " & _
search & " ORDER BY LastName, FirstName"
OleDbDataAdapter1.Fill(DsMembers1)
End Sub
```

Interrupt with DoEvents

In fact, you can usually interrupt an errant program by pressing Ctrl+Alt+Del and terminating it from the Task Manager. It is not a sign of good software, though.

Nothing is worse than accidentally triggering an option that takes a long time, and then not being able to cancel it. Of course, you can reboot the PC, but quality software should not require such drastic measures.

Now, imagine you have a procedure that does lengthy processing in a loop – for example, a routine which calculates how many prime numbers there are up to one million. That takes a significant amount of time. The problem is that while Visual Basic is racing round the loop, the rest of the application is dead. You cannot have a Cancel button, because no Click event will fire until the loop is done. Worse still, if a bug causes an infinite loop, the user will not be able to break in.

Using DoEvents

There are several ways around this problem. The simplest is to use DoEvents. This command hands control back to Windows, so that Click events or other actions can be processed before the loop continues. Here is how to do it:

1 Declare a variable in the Declarations section of the form:

```
Dim CancelFlag as Boolean
```

2 For the button which starts the long process, add the following code (this example uses DoEvents to provide a Cancel button during a lengthy code loop):

If you use DoEvents, there is a possibility that the user may click again on the button which triggers the loop. You should prevent this either by disabling the button (as here) or by setting a flag so that the loop will not run again.

```
Button1.Enabled = False
CancelFlag = False
Try
' code for long operation here
' within the operation regularly
' check this code
Application.DoEvents()
If CancelFlag Then
Label1.Text = "Cancelled"
Exit Sub
End If
' continue with long operation
Finally
Button1.Enabled = True
End Try
```

3 The code for the Cancel button is:

```
CancelFlag=True
```

Where Help files come from

This page does not tell you everything about creating Help files, but gives you an idea of what is involved.

Most professional software comes with Help files. Press F1 in a dialog box, and custom help appears for that dialog.

Microsoft HTML Help workshop is for creating HTML Help files. These consist of HTML pages compiled into a single Help file with a .CHM extension. The Help file includes topics and indexing

Third-party Help software is easier to use and more productive than that supplied by Microsoft. Some software also allows for creating both online Help and a printed manual.

The first step is to build a .CHM Help file for your application. The next step is to set links to the Help file. The easy way to do this is by adding a HelpProvider component to a form. This appears below the form.

The HelpProvider control in the Toolbox

When you add a HelpProvider to a form, you can set its HelpNameSpace to a Help file of your choice. After adding a HelpProvider, other controls on the form get three new properties: HelpKeyword, HelpNavigator and HelpString. Set the HelpNavigator to a type of search in the Help file, such as a topic entry or keyword index. Set the HelpKeyword to the word to search for. If there is no HelpNameSpace set, use the HelpString to create a pop-up F1 help for the control. These are somewhat like a ToolTip, but only appear when the user presses F1.

If you have Web access, visit Microsoft's website for the information about new Help authoring tools.

Setting help properties for a Button control. This only activates when the Button has the focus and the user presses F1

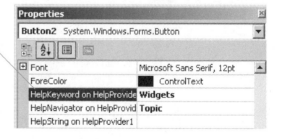

Using a Setup Project

If you find the Package and Deployment Wizard hard to work with, investigate third-party alternatives such as InstallShield or WISE.

When you have completed a Visual Basic application, you will naturally want to distribute it to others. Unfortunately, installing a Windows application is not always straightforward. The main reason is that most applications are dependent on the presence of a number of files, code libraries, and often a database engine. These may be present on your development machine, but not on everyone else's PC. In addition, many files cannot just be copied, but need to be registered in some way. For Visual Basic .Net, it is essential that the .NET Framework runtime files are installed, in the same version as used by your application. Finally, there is the business of adding Start menu or Desktop shortcuts, so that users can find the application.

All this means that you cannot generally just copy an application onto someone else's hard disk and expect it to work. Instead, you need to create a set of installation files which include a Setup application, and copy them to CD or make them available for download on the Web. This application does the work of checking versions, copying files, registering any ActiveX controls and finally installing program shortcuts onto the Start menu. Fortunately, Visual Basic has a wizard which will create this Setup application for you. The following example demonstrates how this works with a simple application, the Interest Calculator created on page 60.

Getting started

It is important to add the Setup project to your project, rather than starting a new solution, since it makes it easier to configure. If you use the Setup wizard, available in some versions of Visual Basic, the same applies.

Having checked that your application is fault-free, compile and save it with the configuration set to Release. Leaving the solution open, choose File > Add Project > New Project.

design] - Form1.vb [De

Window   Help

Release

Add Project   New Project...
Open Solution...   Existing Project...
Close Solution   Existing Project From Web...

2   In the New Project dialog, choose Setup Project and call it Easy
Steps Calculator Setup.

3   Click the
Application
Folder in
the File
System
view.

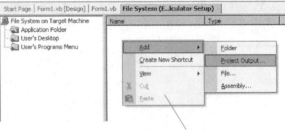

Then right-click in the blank
area to the right, and choose
Add > Project Output.

If your screen does not look
like this, right-click the Setup
project in Solution Explorer,
choose View > File System

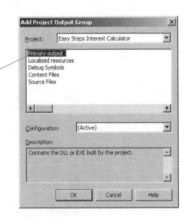

4   In the Project Output dialog,
choose Primary Output and
click OK. If you have other
files such as Help files or
bitmaps, right-click again and
choose Add File.

5   In the Solution Explorer,
notice how the .NET runtime
is listed under Detected
Dependencies. This is a
warning that your project
may not run unless other files
are added. Right-click the
project name and choose
Add > Merge Module.

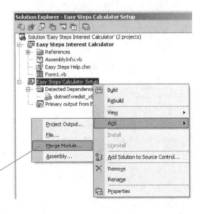

...cont'd

The exact list of merge modules will vary depending on what is installed on your machine. A merge module is a packaged setup routine that can be inserted into another setup routine.

The currently active folder is distinguished by a slightly different icon, showing an open folder. The "User's Program Menu" refers to the Programs section of the Start Menu. If you want to access other special folders, such as the top level of the Start Menu, right-click the File System panel and choose Add Special Folder.

The Setup also creates an uninstall program. You can see this after running the Setup, in the Add/Remove Programs part of Control Panel.

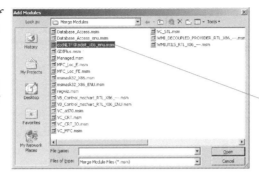

6. In the list of Merge Modules, choose the module with a name beginning dotNetFXRedist and click Open. This is the runtime for the .NET Framework.

7. Now return to the File System view. In the left-hand panel, select User's Programs Menu. In the right-hand panel, right-click and choose Create New Shortcut.

8. In the Select Item in Project dialog, double-click the Application Folder and then select the Primary Output. Click OK.

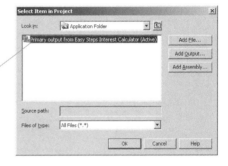

9. Rename the Shortcut to Easy Steps Calculator. This is the

name that will appear on the Start menu, and the user is unlikely to understand the term Primary Output.

10. From the Build menu, choose to Build the setup project. You can also right-click the Project name in Solution Explorer and choose Build.

11. The compiled Setup.exe is in the Release folder in the project directory. Distribute all the files in this directory to your users.

More about the Setup Project

The step-by-step guide explained the minimum steps to create a setup routine for an application. However, you may want to further enhance the project. For example, the wording on the dialogs could be improved. Here is some more information about the Setup project:

The Windows Installer

The full InstallShield product has extra tools, such as a visual dialog editor for the Setup dialogs.

The Setup Project generates files that are run by the Windows Installer service. This is a sophisticated and highly complex feature of Windows. The reason for the complexity of the Setup Project is the complexity of the Windows Installer itself. In addition, the Setup Project uses tools developed by a third-party vendor, InstallShield.

Setup Project Views

The Setup Project has several views. These are as follows:

- **File System:** This is where the actual files to be installed are determined. This view is like a virtual Windows Explorer, where you add files in the location where they are to be placed on the target machine. It is important to use the Special folders, since you cannot know in advance how the target machine is configured. Special folders read the location of items like the Start menu, or My Documents folder, when the setup runs

- **Registry:** This view looks like Regedit but with an empty registry. You can add registry entries, and they will be replicated on the user's machine

Making an application open a document on double-click can be complex, particularly if your application might already be running.

- **File Type:** This is important for applications that use documents. Normally, you would create a new File Type for your document. You can associate commands with the File Type, so that when the user double-clicks a document, it opens in your application

- **User Interface:** This is the series of dialogs seen by the user. The Administrative Install is used to install setup files to a network location, from which other users can install it. When you are getting started with the installer, concentrate on the main Install sequence

- **Custom actions:** These are external scripts or executables that you can run as part of the install process. This can be a life-saver if you cannot get the Installer's built-in functions to do exactly what you require

- **Launch conditions:** You may want installation to fail in some circumstances, for example if the user has too little RAM for your application to run properly. Another aspect is whether the user might already have a later version of the application. Adding a check for this prevents trouble

To understand how the Setup Project works, it is worth reading the section on the Windows Installer in online Help.

Customizing the Setup Project

Most Setup features are accessed by right-click menus and by setting properties in the Properties Window. Have the Properties Window open, and click an item in one of the views to see the available properties.

Here is how to modify the dialog wording in the example Setup:

You can also add new dialogs. Right-click the Install sequence and choose Add Dialog. Simple options include a Readme dialog and a user license display.

In the Solution Explorer, select the Setup Project Name and press F4. The Deployment Project Properties are displayed. Amend the ProductName and Title, for example to remove the word Setup. These variables are used throughout the project

Display the User Interface view and select the Welcome dialog. In the Properties Window, modify the WelcomeText. You can use variables like [ProductName] in square brackets. Build and test the customised project

Where next?

You have come to the end of *Visual Basic .Net in easy steps*, but there is plenty more to learn and achieve. Here are some tips:

1. Start a project

It is hard to learn how to program if you have no clear goal. Find a project, whether at home, in the office, or at a club, and work out how to use Visual Basic to create a solution. Even if your first attempt is not completely successful, you will learn a lot by solving the real-world problems it throws up.

When you look for help on Visual Basic, make sure you specify Visual Basic .Net. It is very different from older versions.

2. Get help

Whatever problem you have, the chances are that someone, somewhere has tackled it before. Because Visual Basic is so popular, you can easily find help in books and on the Internet. Microsoft runs Internet newsgroups on Visual Basic, where you can ask questions.

3. Test and improve

In business, the customer is always right. In software, the user is always right. If your Visual Basic program is to be used by others, get them to try it out and report back the problems they have. Even better, watch them working and see how you can make the software more productive, by cutting down the number of steps needed to perform some task, or improving the screen layout, or speeding performance at critical points.

Don't ignore the most obvious source of help: Visual Basic's online reference

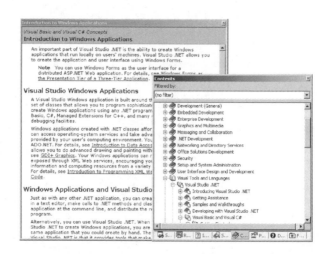

Index

.Net Framework   9

D

E

F